50 garter stitch gifts to knit

50
garter stitch gifts to knit

THE ULTIMATE EASY-TO-KNIT COLLECTION

FEATURING UNIVERSAL YARN DELUXE WORSTED

THE EDITORS OF SIXTH&SPRING BOOKS

sixth&springbooks
NEW YORK

sixth&spring
books
161 Avenue of the Americas
New York, NY 10013
SIXTHANDSPRINGBOOKS.COM

MANAGING EDITOR
LAURA COOKE

SENIOR EDITOR
LISA SILVERMAN

ART DIRECTOR
DIANE LAMPHRON

YARN EDITOR
VANESSA PUTT

EDITORIAL ASSISTANT
JOHANNA LEVY

GRAPHIC DESIGNER
ARETA BUK

SUPERVISING
PATTERNS EDITOR
LORI STEINBERG

PATTERNS EDITOR
RENEE LORION

STYLIST
JOANNA RADOW

PHOTOGRAPHER
JACK DEUTSCH

STYLIST'S ASSISTANT
KATHY VILLALON

HAIR AND MAKEUP
INGEBORG
SOKPHALLA BAN

VICE PRESIDENT
TRISHA MALCOLM

PUBLISHER
CARRIE KILMER

PRODUCTION
MANAGER
DAVID JOINNIDES

PRESIDENT
ART JOINNIDES

CHAIRMAN
JAY STEIN

Library of Congress Cataloging-in-Publication Data

50 garter stitch gifts to knit : the ultimate easy-knit collection/the editors of Sixth&Spring Books.—First edition.
    pages cm
ISBN 978-1-936096-88-6
1. Knitting—Patterns. 2. Dress accessories. 3. Knitwear. I. Sixth & Spring Books. II. Title: Fifty garter stitch gifts to knit.
TT825.A12389 2015
746.43'2—dc23
                    2014030433

MANUFACTURED IN CHINA

1 3 5 7 9 10 8 6 4 2

First Edition

www.universalyarn.com

Contents

Knitted Treasures

Preface

2015 marks our tenth anniversary here at Universal Yarn. Begun in 2005 by Hal Ozbelli, the company has grown and expanded in many ways over the past decade. Many customers know us for on-trend yarns such as fur, brushed yarns, sequins, and more. Others think of Universal when choosing just the right soft yarn for a baby blanket or sweater. Our lines of self-shading yarns stand out on the shelves, bathed in color and beauty. We also have our luxurious Fibra Natura line of natural yarns, including linen, llama, wool, and cotton blends.

But on top of the vast expanse of specialty products, Universal Yarn is prouder than ever of our Deluxe collection of wools. Worsted-weight wool is a staple for knitters around the world, and Deluxe is the best of the best: a high-quality wool at an affordable price. An ever-expanding palette includes well over 100 solids, 20-plus heathered colors, and natural, undyed varieties. Machine-washable Deluxe Worsted Superwash, also available in a DK weight, is our most recent addition to the family. With more than 50 colors and counting, Superwash has become a favorite of those desiring a natural wool yarn but needing an easy-care finished object.

Universal Yarn is delighted to be partnering with Sixth&Spring Books for the second time. *50 Knitted Gifts for Year-Round Giving* featured the Deluxe family in many adorable, giftable projects, and this follow-up volume celebrating garter stitch could not be a more perfect match of yarn to theme. Simple garter stitch is what most of us knitters learned to do first. Although garter stitch can be "riffed" on in so many ways, it is fundamentally the most basic way of knitting. Garter stitch and Deluxe Worsted: back to basics all around!

We graciously acknowledge the collaborative effort of all the contributing designers to *50 Garter Stitch Gifts to Knit*. It is through your creative eyes that we are able to see all that garter stitch and Deluxe Worsted can be.

Amy Gunderson & Yonca Ozbelli
Universal Yarn

The Projects

Graphic Mosaic Cowl

The use of black and white plays up the geometric lines of a mosaic pattern created with slipped stitches on this head-turning accessory.

Designed by Susan Lowman

KNITTED MEASUREMENTS
Circumference 60"/152.5cm
Length 8"/20.5cm

MATERIALS
■ Two 3½oz/100g skeins (each approx 220yd/201m) of Universal Yarn *Deluxe Worsted* (100% wool) each in #1900 ebony (A) and #12257 pulp (B)

■ Size 7 (4.5mm) circular needle, 40"/100cm long, OR SIZE TO OBTAIN GAUGE

■ Stitch marker

GAUGE
22 sts and 40 rows = 4"/10cm over mosaic st pat using size 7 (4.5mm) needles.
TAKE TIME TO CHECK GAUGE.

MOSAIC PATTERN STITCH
(multiple of 10 sts)
Rnd 1 With B, *[k3, sl 1] twice, k1, sl 1; rep from * around.
Rnd 2 With B, *[p3, sl 1] twice, p1, sl 1; rep from * around.
Rnd 3 With A, *sl 1, k5, sl 1, k3; rep from * around.
Rnd 4 With A, *sl 1, p5, sl 1, p3; rep from * around.
Rnd 5 With B, *k1, sl 1, k3, sl 1, k4; rep from * around.
Rnd 6 With B, *p1, sl 1, p3, sl 1, p4; rep from * around.
Rnd 7 With A, *k2, sl 1, k1, sl 1, k3, sl 1, k1; rep from * around.
Rnd 8 With A, *p2, sl 1, p1, sl 1, p3, sl 1, p1; rep from * around.
Rnds 9 and 10 Rep rnds 5 and 6.
Rnds 11 and 12 Rep rnds 3 and 4.
Rnds 13 and 14 Rep rnds 1 and 2.
Rnds 15 and 16 Rep rnds 7 and 8.
Rnds 17 and 18 Rep rnds 5 and 6.
Rnds 19 and 20 Rep rnds 7 and 8.
Rep rnds 1–20 for mosaic pat st.

COWL
With A, cast on 330 sts. Join, being careful not to twist sts, and place marker for beg of rnd.
Work 4 rnds in garter st (k 1 rnd, p 1 rnd).

BEGIN MOSAIC ST PAT
Rnd 1 Work 10-st rep of mosaic st pat 33 times around.
Cont to work in this manner until rnd 20 is complete. Rep rnds 1–20 twice more, then rnds 1–14 once.
With A, work 4 rnds in garter st.
Bind off. ■

Happy Blocks Baby Blanket

Intarsia blocks worked in six cheerful colors pop against a neutral gray background in a fun, modern design.

Designed by Kennita Tully

KNITTED MEASUREMENTS
26 x 31"/66 x 78.5cm

MATERIALS
■ Three 3½oz/100g skeins (each approx 220yd/201m) of Universal Yarn *Deluxe Worsted Superwash* (100% wool) in #733 sweatshirt grey (A)

■ 1 skein each in #702 autumn orange (B), #716 nitrox blue (C), #721 honeysuckle (D), #709 lime tree (E), #720 grape taffy (F), and #705 orangesicle (G)

■ One pair size 7 (4.5mm) needles OR SIZE TO OBTAIN GAUGE

■ Size 7 (4.5mm) crochet hook

■ Bobbins

GAUGE
17 sts and 33 rows = 4"/10cm over garter st using size 7 (4.5mm) needles. TAKE TIME TO CHECK GAUGE.

CROCHET CAST-ON
1) Make a slip knot and place on hook.
2) Hold hook in front of knitting needle with the working yarn behind the knitting needle.
3) With crochet hook, draw a loop through the slip knot. The yarn around the knitting needle forms the first cast-on st. Keeping the new loop on the crochet hook, move the working yarn to the back of the needle. Cont to form sts in this manner, drawing each loop through the new loop on the crochet hook, until there is 1 less st on the needle than the desired number of cast-on sts.
4) Place the loop from the crochet hook on the needle to form the last cast-on st.

NOTES
1) Blanket is worked using the intarsia method. Use a separate bobbin for each color section; do not carry colors across the back.
2) When changing colors, twist strands on WS to avoid holes.
3) Sl the first st and purl the last st of every row.
4) Circular needle is used to accommodate large number of sts. Do not join.

BLANKET
With crochet hook and A, cast on 112 sts using the crochet cast-on method.
Next row Sl 1, k to last st, p1.
Rep this row 19 times more for garter st.

*Next row (RS) Sl 1, k9, k12 B, k4 A, k12 C, k4 A, k12 D, k4 A, k12 E, k4 A, k12 F, k4 A, k12 G, with A k to the last st, p1.
Next row Sl 1, k in colors as they appear to the last st, p1.
Rep last 2 rows 11 times more.***
With A, work 8 rows in garter st.
Next row (RS) Sl 1, k9, k12 D, k4 A, k12 E, k4 A, k12 F, k4 A, k12 G, k4 A, k12 B, k4 A, k12 C, with A k to the last st, p1.
Next row Sl 1, k in colors as they appear to the last st, p1.
Rep last 2 rows 11 times more.
With A, work 8 rows in garter st.
Next row (RS) Sl 1, k9, k12 F, k4 A, k12 G, k4 A, k12 B, k4 A, k12 C, k4 A, k12 D, k4 A, k12 E, with A k to the last st, p1.
Next row Sl 1, k in colors as they appear to the last st, p1.**
Rep last 2 rows 11 times more.
With A, work 8 rows in garter st.
Rep from * to ** once more, then rep from * to ***.
With A, work 20 rows. Bind off. ■

Semicircle Shawl

Turn heads in an oversize shawl worked multi-directionally using short rows and intarsia to create a graphic statement of shape and color.

◆

Designed by Amy Gunderson

KNITTED MEASUREMENTS
Width along upper edge 64"/162.5cm
Length 32"/81cm

MATERIALS
■ Four 3½oz/100g skeins (each approx 220yd/201m) of Universal Yarn *Deluxe Worsted* (100% wool) in #12192 nitrox blue (A)

■ 2 skeins each in #12501 oatmeal heather (B) and #13109 stone (C)

■ Size 7 (4.5mm) circular needle, 40"/100cm long, OR SIZE TO OBTAIN GAUGE

■ One set (2) size 7 (4.5mm) double-pointed needles (dpns) for I-cord edging

GAUGE
16 sts and 32 rows = 4"/10cm over garter st using size 7 (4.5mm) needles. TAKE TIME TO CHECK GAUGE.

SHORT ROW WRAP & TURN (W&T)
on RS row (on WS row)
1) Wyib (wyif), sl next st purlwise.
2) Move yarn between the needles to the front (back).
3) Sl the same st back to LH needle. Turn work. One st is wrapped.

4) When working the wrapped st, insert RH needle under the wrap and work it tog with the corresponding st on needle to hide or close wrap.

KNITTED CAST-ON
(at beg or end of a row)
1) Draw yarn through the next st to make a new st, but do not drop the st from the LH needle.
2) Slip the new st to the LH needle. Rep steps 1 and 2 until the desired number of sts has been cast on.

NOTES
1) Slip all sts purlwise with yarn held to WS of work.
2) Use a separate bobbin for each color section. Do not carry colors across WS of work.
3) Twist strands on WS when changing colors to avoid holes in work.
4) Shawl is worked from the lower edge to the neck edge.

SHAWL
SECTION 1
With A, cast on 15 sts; with B, cast on 42 sts—57 sts.
Set-up row (WS) With B, sl 1, k41; with A, k14, sl 1.
Row 1 (RS) With A, k15; with B, k42.
Row 2 With B, sl 1, k41; with A, k14, sl 1.
Rows 3 and 4 Rep rows 1 and 2.
Row 5 With A, k15; with B, k28, w&t.
Row 6 With B, k28; with A, k14, sl 1.

Row 7 With A, k14; with B, k15, w&t.
Row 8 With B, k15; with A, k14, sl 1.
Row 9 With A, k14, w&t.
Row 10 With A, k13, sl 1.
Row 11 With A, k15, hiding wraps; with B, k42, hiding wraps.
Row 12 With B, sl 1, k41; with A, k14, sl 1.
Rows 13–16 With A, sl 1, k56.
Row 17 With A, k15; with B, k42.
Row 18 With B, sl 1, k41; with A, k14, sl 1.
Rows 19–22 Rep rows 13–16.
Rep rows 3–22 for 39 times more, then rep rows 3–12.
Next row (RS) With A, k15; with B, k42.
Next row With B, sl 1, k41; with A, k14, sl 1.
Bind off as foll: With A, bind off 14 sts purlwise, with B, bind off rem sts purlwise.

SECTION 2
With RS facing and C, pick up and k 284 sts evenly along shorter side edge of section 1.
Set-up row (WS) Sl 1, k to last st, sl 1.
Row 1 (dec RS) K1, *k2tog, k5; rep from * to last 3 sts, k2tog, k1—243 sts.
Row 2 Sl 1, k to last st, sl 1.
Row 3 Knit.
Rep rows 2 and 3 for 5 times more, then rep row 2 once.
Next (dec) row (RS) K7, *k2tog, k4; rep from * to last 8 sts, k2tog, k6—204 sts.
Next row Sl 1, k to last st, sl 1. Break C.

Next row With B, knit.

Next row Sl 1, k to last st, sl 1.
Rep last 2 rows once more. Break B.

Next row (RS) With A, knit.

SECTION 3

Next row (RS) Using knitted cast-on method and A, cast on 7 sts; with C, cast on 17 sts—228 sts.

Set-up row (WS) With C; sl 1, k16; With A, k6, k2tog tbl (1 st from section 3 with 1 st from section 2), turn.

Row 1 (RS) With A, sl 1, k6; with C, k17.

Row 2 With C; sl 1, k16; With A, k6, k2tog tbl, turn.

Row 3 With A, sl 1, k23.

Row 4 With A, sl 1, k22, k2tog tbl, turn.

Rows 5 and 6 Rep rows 3 and 4.

Rows 7 and 8 Rep rows 1 and 2.

Row 9 With A, sl 1, k6; with C, k11, w&t.

Row 10 With C, k11; with A, k6, k2tog tbl, turn.

Row 11 With A, sl 1, k6; with C, k5, w&t.

Row 12 With C, k5, with A, k6, k2tog tbl, turn.

Row 13 With A, sl 1, k5, w&t.

Row 14 With A, k5, k2tog tbl, turn.

Row 15 With A, sl 1, k6, hiding wraps; with C, k17, hiding wraps.

Row 16 With C, sl 1, k16; with A, k6, k2tog tbl, turn.

Rows 17–20 Rep rows 3–6.

Rows 21 and 22 Rep rows 1 and 2.
Rep rows 3–22 for 19 times more.

Next row (RS) With A, sl 1, k6; with C, k17.

Next row With C, bind off 17 sts knitwise; with A, bind off 6 sts knitwise, k3tog. Fasten off rem st.

SECTION 4

With RS facing and B, pick up and k 144 sts evenly along shorter side edge of section 3.

Set-up row (WS) Sl 1, k to last st, sl 1.

Row 1 (RS) Knit.

Row 2 Sl 1, k to last st, sl 1.

Rows 3–6 Rep rows 1 and 2 twice more.

Row 7 (dec RS) K1, k2tog, k3, *k2tog, k5; rep from * to last 5 sts, k2tog, k3—123 sts.

Row 8 Rep row 2. Break B.

Rows 9–12 With C, rep rows 1 and 2 twice. Break C, change to A.

SECTION 5

Row 1 (RS) Knit.

Row 2 Sl 1, k to last st, sl 1.

Row 3 (dec) K5, *k2tog, k6; rep from * to last 6 sts, k2tog, k4—108 sts.

Row 4 Rep row 2.

Rows 5–10 Rep rows 1 and 2 for 3 times.

Row 11 (dec RS) K1, k2tog, k2, *k2tog, k5; rep from * to last 5 sts, k2, k2tog, k1—92 sts.

Rows 12–18 Rep rows 4–10.

Row 19 (dec RS) K3, *k2tog, k4; rep from * to last 5 sts, k2tog, k3—77 sts.

Rows 20–26 Rep rows 4–10.

Row 27 (dec RS) K1, [k2tog, k3] 6 times, [k2tog, k2] 3 times, k2tog, k1, [k2tog, k2] twice [k2tog, k3] 4 times, k2tog, k1—60 sts.

Rows 28–34 Rep rows 4–10.

Row 35 (dec RS) K1, *k2tog, k2; rep from * to last 3 sts, k2tog, k1—45 sts.

Rows 36–42 Rep rows 4–10.

Row 43 (dec RS) K2, *k2tog, k1; rep from * to last 4 sts, k2tog, k2—31 sts.

Rows 44–50 Rep rows 4–10.

Row 51 (dec RS) K1, *k2tog; rep from * to last 2 sts, k2—17 sts.

Row 52 Rep row 2.

Rows 53–56 Rep rows 1 and 2 twice.

Row 57 (dec RS) K2, [k2tog] 7 times, k1—10 sts.

Row 58 Rep row 2.

Rows 59 and 60 Rep rows 1 and 2.

Row 61 (dec RS) Ssk, [k2tog] 4 times—5 sts.

Row 62 Rep row 2.

Row 63 (dec RS) Ssk, k1, k2tog—3 sts.

Next row SK2P. Fasten off.

FINISHING
EDGING

With dpn and C, cast on 3 sts. Beg at one corner with RS facing, work applied I-cord evenly around entire edge of shawl as foll: *With C, k2; with A, pick up and k 1 st along edge of shawl; with C, k2tog tbl (last C st, with picked-up A st). Slide sts to opposite end of needle to work next row from RS; rep from * to next corner, work 2 rows of I-cord without joining, then rep from * to beg of edging. Work 2 rows of I-cord without joining. Bind off. Sew ends of edging tog. ■

Colorwork Cardi

A slip stitch pattern forms a charming colorwork design in the yoke of this cardigan knit from the top down.

◆

Designed by Pat Olski

SIZES
Small, Medium, Large, X-Large, and XX-Large
Shown in size Small

KNITTED MEASUREMENTS
Bust 38½ (40½, 42½, 44½, 46½)"/97.5 (103, 108, 113, 118)cm
Length 19¼ (21½, 22½, 22½, 22½)"/49 (54.5, 57, 57, 57)cm
Upper arm 11¾ (12¼, 13¼, 13¾, 14¼)"/30 (31, 33.5, 35, 36)cm

MATERIALS
■ 3 (3, 4, 4, 4) 3½oz/100g skeins (each approx 220yd/201m) of Universal Yarn *Deluxe Worsted* (100% wool) in #13109 stone (MC)

■ 1 skein each in #12288 bashful pink (A), #12506 azure heather (B), #3620 coral (C), #12504 pomegranate heather (D), and #12224 chartreuse olive (E)

■ One size 8 (5mm) circular needle, 24"/60cm long, OR SIZE TO OBTAIN GAUGE

■ Seven ¾"/2cm buttons

■ Stitch holders

■ Stitch markers in different colors

GAUGE
16 sts and 34 rows = 4"/10cm over garter st using size 8 (5mm) needles.
TAKE TIME TO CHECK GAUGE.

SLIP STITCH STRIPE
Row 1 (RS) With Color 1, knit.
Row 2 (WS) With Color 1, *sl 1 wyif, k1; rep from * to end.
Row 3 With Color 2, k the knit sts and sl the sl sts wyib.
Row 4 Rep row 3.
Rows 5 and 6 With Color 1, knit.
Rep rows 1–6 for slip stitch stripe.

STRIPE SEQUENCE
Working in slip stitch stripe, work sequence as follows (Color 1, 2):
Stripe 1: A, B
Stripe 2: B, C
Stripe 3: C, B
Stripe 4: D, E
Stripe 5: E, A

NOTE
Cardigan is worked from the top down in rows. Circular needle is used to accommodate large number of sts.
Do not join.

CARDIGAN
With MC, cast on 51 sts.
Row 1 (WS) K1, place marker (pm), k2, pm in 2nd color, k7 for sleeve, pm in 2nd color, k2, pm, k27 for back, pm, k2, pm in 2nd color, k7 for sleeve, pm in 2nd color, k2, pm, k1.

Row 2 (inc RS) Kfb, M1, sl marker, k2, sl marker, M1, k7, M1, sl marker, k2, sl marker, M1, k27, M1, sl marker, k2, sl marker, M1, k7, M1, sl marker, k2, sl marker, M1, kfb—61 sts.
Row 3 Knit.
Row 4 (inc RS) Kfb, k to marker, M1, [sl marker, k2, sl marker, M1, k to marker, M1] 3 times, sl marker, k2, sl marker, M1, k to last st, kfb—10 sts inc'd.
Row 5 Knit.
Row 6 Kfb, k to last st, kfb—2 sts inc'd.
Row 7 Knit.
Rep rows 4–7 five times more—133 sts.
Row 28 (inc RS) Cast on 5 sts for button band, work as for row 4 to end, cast on 5 sts at end of row for button band—153 sts.
Rows 29–31 Knit to last st, sl 1 (selvage st).
Row 32 With E, k to marker, M1, sl marker, k2, sl marker, k to marker, sl marker, k2, sl marker, M1, k to marker, M1, sl marker, k2, sl marker, k to marker, sl marker, k2, sl marker, M1, k to last st, sl 1—157 sts (raglan inc's worked at front and back edges only).
Row 33 With E, knit to last st, sl 1.

BEG STRIPE SEQUENCE AND BUTTONHOLES
Note Read before cont to knit. Shaping continues as stripe sequence AND buttonholes are worked. Cont to sl last st of every row as selvage st.

Working first and last 5 sts of every row in garter st (k every row) for button band, work 5 stripes in stripe sequence, AT THE SAME TIME, cont to work raglan shaping by working inc's for fronts and back every 4th row 10 (12, 14, 12, 10) times more, then every other row 0 (0, 0, 4, 8) times more, and for sleeves (inside 2nd color markers) every 4th row 0 (0, 0, 0, 3) times, then every 6th row 7 (8, 9, 10, 8) times more, AT THE SAME TIME, work buttonhole on next RS row, then every 20th (22nd, 22nd, 22nd, 22nd) row 6 times more, as foll: work in pat to last 6 sts, k2tog, yo, k3, sl 1.

When stripe sequence is complete, work 2 rows in A, 8 rows in MC—225 (237, 249, 261, 273) sts when all shaping is complete, 39 (41, 43, 45, 47) for each front, 37 (39, 41, 43, 45) for each sleeve, 65 (69, 73, 77, 81) for the back, and 2 sts between each of the 4 raglan markers.

DIVIDE BODY AND SLEEVES

Note Remove markers as they are passed on next row.

Next row (RS) K39 (41, 43, 45, 47), k 1 raglan st, place next 39 (41, 43, 45, 47) sts (sleeve sts plus 1 raglan st each side) on st holder, cast on 10 sts for underarm, k 1 raglan st, k65 (69, 73, 77, 81) for back, k 1 raglan st, place next 39 (41, 43, 45, 47) sts on st holder, cast on 10 sts for underarm, k 1 raglan st, k to end—39 (41, 43, 45, 47) sts on holders for each sleeve, 167 (175, 183, 191, 199) sts for body. Cont in garter st over body sts until all 7 buttonholes have been worked, then k 10 rows more. Body measures approx 10½ (12, 12, 12, 12)"/26.5 (30.5, 30.5, 30.5, 30.5)cm from underarm. Bind off.

SLEEVES

With MC, cast on 1 st, beg at center of cast-on sts at underarm, pick up and k 5 sts, k 39 (41, 43, 45, 47) sts from holder, pick up and k 5 sts along underarm,

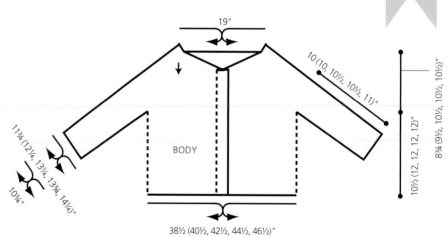

cast on 1 st—51 (53, 55, 57, 59) sts. Knit 14 (14, 16, 16, 18) rows. Dec 1 st each side, 2 sts in from edge, on next row, then rep dec row every 10th row 3 (4, 5, 6, 7) times more—43 sts. Work even until sleeve measures 10 (10, 10½,

10½, 11)"/25.5 (25.5, 26.5, 26.5, 28)cm, end with a WS row. Bind off.

FINISHING

Block lightly to measurements. Sew buttons to band opposite buttonholes. ■

Hole in One Cowl

The designer incorporates her one-of-a-kind Geometric Openwork™ technique into a wide, drapey striped cowl that's knit in two directions.

Designed by Cornelia Tuttle Hamilton

KNITTED MEASUREMENTS
Circumference 44"/111.5cm
Length 11¾"/30cm

MATERIALS
■ One 3½oz/100g skein (each approx 220yd/201m) of Universal Yarn *Deluxe Worsted* (100% wool) in #12287 cerise (A), #12236 violet glow (B), #12288 bashful pink (C), #12275 mulberry (D), and #14018 rhapsody (E)

■ Size 7 (4.5mm) circular needle, 29"/74cm long, OR SIZE TO OBTAIN GAUGE

GAUGE
20 sts and 40 rows = 4"/10cm over garter st using size 7 (4.5mm) needles. TAKE TIME TO CHECK GAUGE.

BACKWARD LOOP CAST-ON METHOD

1) Place a slip knot on the RH needle, leaving a short tail. Wrap the yarn from the ball around your left thumb from front to back and secure it in your palm with your other fingers.

2) Insert the needle upward through the strand on your thumb.

3) Slip this loop from your thumb onto the needle, pulling the yarn from the ball to tighten it. Cont in this way until the desired number of sts has been cast on.

STRIPE SEQUENCE

*A, B, C, D, E; rep from * for stripe sequence.

NOTES

1) Cowl is worked in 2 sections; the horizontal section is worked first, then the vertical section is worked on sts picked up and knit along the side of the horizontal section.

2) Use the backward loop method to cast on stitches within the pattern rows.

3) Circular needle is used to accommodate large number of sts. Do not join.

COWL

HORIZONTAL SECTION

With A, cast on 116 sts.
Knit 6 rows. Break yarn. Change to B.
**Next row (WS) K4, bind off 4 sts, k3 (4 sts on needle, including the loop from the bind-off); rep from * to end.
Next (pattern) row (RS) [K4, turn] 9 times, *cast on 4 sts using the backward loop method, [k4, turn] 4 times, drop last cast-on st from RH needle, with RH needle under the strand of the dropped st, k1, pass strand over this st, k3, turn, [k4, turn] 3 times, drop last cast-on st from RH needle, with RH needle under the strand of the dropped st, k1, pass strand over this st, k3, turn; rep from * across entire row.
Knit 6 rows over all sts. Break yarn.
Change to next color. Cont in color sequence, rep from ** for stripe 6 times more. Bind off.

VERTICAL STRIPE SECTION

With RS facing and E, pick up and k 28 sts along one side edge of horizontal stripe section. Knit 6 rows.
Next row (WS) K4, bind off 4 sts, k3; rep from * to end.
Beg with A, cont in stripe sequence and work as for horizontal section until 13 more stripes have been worked. Bind off.

FINISHING

Sew bound-off edge of vertical stripe section to opposite edge of horizontal stripe section to form a tube. ■

Simply Striped Mitts

Make these easy but elegant mitts your own: choose tonal shades for a subtle style or bright, contrasting colors for a more lively look.

Designed by Cheryl Murray

SIZE
Adult woman

KNITTED MEASUREMENTS
Palm circumference 7½"/19cm
Length 9½"/24cm

MATERIALS
■ One 3½oz/100g skein (each approx 220yd/201m) of Universal Yarn *Deluxe Worsted* (100% wool) each in #3692 Christmas green (A) and #13102 husk (B)

■ One set (5) size 6 (4mm) double-pointed needles (dpns) OR SIZE TO OBTAIN GAUGE

■ Stitch markers

■ Scrap yarn

GAUGE
20 sts and 40 rnds = 4"/10cm over garter stripe pat using size 6 (4mm) needles.
TAKE TIME TO CHECK GAUGE.

GARTER STRIPE PATTERN
Rnd 1 With B, knit.
Rnd 2 With A, purl.
Rep rnds 1 and 2 for garter stripe pat.

MITT
CUFF
With A, cast on 40 sts. Divide evenly on dpns. Join, being careful not to twist, and place marker (pm) for beg of rnd.
Beg with a knit rnd, work 5 rnds in garter st (k 1 rnd, p 1 rnd).
Next (dec) rnd P2tog, p to end—39 sts.

BEGIN GARTER STRIPE PAT
Work in garter stripe pat, rep dec rnd every 6th rnd 3 times more—36 sts.
Cont in garter stripe pat until piece measures 5"/12.5cm from beg, end with a rnd 2.

SHAPE GUSSET
Next (inc) rnd K17, pm, M1, k2, M1, pm, k to end of rnd—38 sts.
Work 5 rnds more in garter stripe pat.
Next (inc) rnd K to marker, sl marker, M1, k to next marker, M1, sl marker, k to end of rnd—2 sts inc'd.
Cont in garter stripe pat as established, rep inc rnd every 6th rnd 3 times more—12 gusset sts between markers, 46 sts in rnd. Work even until piece measures 7½"/19cm from beg, end with a row 2.
Next rnd K17, place 12 gusset sts on scrap yarn for thumb, cast on 2 sts, k to end of rnd.
Work even in pat on 36 sts until piece measures 9"/23cm from beg. Break B.

With A only, work 5 rnds in garter st. Bind off loosely purlwise.

THUMB
Place 12 thumb sts on dpns, with A, pick up and k 2 sts along thumb opening—14 sts.
Pm for beg of rnd, and work 5 rnds in garter st. Bind off loosely. ■

With Warm Wishes

Zigzag Mosaic Scarf

In a clever use of color, a mosaic pattern overlaps chevrons and straight stripes in a scarf that's worked sideways.

Designed by EJ Slayton

KNITTED MEASUREMENTS
6 x 48"/15 x 122cm

MATERIALS
■ One 3½oz/100g skein (each approx 220yd/201m) of Universal Yarn *Deluxe Worsted* (100% wool) each in #13112 red apple (MC), #12503 charcoal heather (A), and #12502 smoke heather (B)

■ One size 7 (4.5mm) circular needle, 24"/60cm long, OR SIZE TO OBTAIN GAUGE

GAUGE
17 sts and 38 rows = 4"/10cm over mosaic pattern using size 7 (4.5mm) needles.
TAKE TIME TO CHECK GAUGE.

NOTES
1) Sl all sts purlwise with yarn in back on RS rows, with yarn in front on WS rows.
2) Carry unused colors along edge; cut A and B only when changing background color after rows 14 and 42.
3) Scarf is worked from edge to edge. Circular needle is used to accommodate large number of sts, do not join.

MOSAIC PATTERN
(multiple of 14 sts plus 3)
Row 1 (RS) With MC, k1, *[k1, sl 1] 3 times, k3, sl 1, [k1, sl 1] twice; rep from * to last 2 sts, k2.
Row 2 K2, *sl 1, [k1, sl 1] twice, k3, [sl 1, k1] 3 times; rep from * to last st, k1.
Row 3 With CC, k1, *k6, sl 1, k1, sl 1, k5; rep from * to last 2 sts, k2.
Row 4 K2, *k5, sl 1, k1, sl 1, k6; rep from * to last st, k1.
Row 5 With MC, k1, *[k1, sl 1] twice, k7, sl 1, k1, sl 1; rep from * to last 2 sts, k2.
Row 6 K2, *sl 1, k1, sl 1, k7, [sl 1, k1] twice; rep from * to last st, k1.
Row 7 With CC, k1, *k4, sl 1, [k1, sl 1] 3 times, k3; rep from * to last 2 sts, k2.
Row 8 K2, *k3, sl 1, [k1, sl 1] 3 times, k4; rep from * to last st, k1.
Row 9 With MC, k1, *k1, sl 1, k11, sl 1; rep from * to last 2 sts, k2.
Row 10 K2, *sl 1, k11, sl 1, k1; rep from * to last st, k1.
Row 11 With CC, k1, *k2, sl 1, [k1, sl 1] 5 times, k1; rep from * to last 2 sts, k2.
Row 12 K2, *k1, sl 1, [k1, sl 1] 5 times, k2; rep from * to last st, k1.
Rows 13 and 14 With MC, knit.
Row 15 With CC, k1, *[k1, sl 1] 3 times, k3, sl 1, [k1, sl 1] twice; rep from * to last 2 sts, k2.
Row 16 K2, *sl 1, [k1, sl 1] twice, k3, [sl 1, k1] 3 times; rep from * to last st, k1.
Row 17 With MC, k1, *k6, sl 1, k1, sl 1, k5; rep from * to last 2 sts, k2.
Row 18 K2, *k5, sl 1, k1, sl 1, k6; rep from * to last st, k1.
Row 19 With CC, k1, *[k1, sl 1] twice, k7, sl 1, k1, sl 1; rep from * to last 2 sts, k2.
Row 20 K2, *sl 1, k1, sl 1, k7, [sl 1, k1] twice; rep from * to last st, k1.
Row 21 With MC, k1, *k4, sl 1, [k1, sl 1] 3 times, k3; rep from * to last 2 sts, k2.
Row 22 K2, *k3, sl 1, [k1, sl 1] 3 times, k4; rep from * to last st, k1.
Row 23 With CC, k1, *k1, sl 1, k11, sl 1; rep from * to last 2 sts, k2.
Row 24 K2, *sl 1, k11, sl 1, k1; rep from * to last st, k1.
Row 25 With MC, k1, *k2, sl 1, [k1, sl 1] 5 times, k1; rep from * to last 2 sts, k2.
Row 26 K2, *k1, sl 1, [k1, sl 1] 5 times, k2; rep from * to last st, k1.
Rows 27 and 28 With CC, knit.
Rep rows 1–28 for mosaic pat, using A or B for CC as indicated below.

SCARF
With A, cast on 213 sts. Knit 3 rows. With MC, beg mosaic pat, working contrast colors as foll:
Rows 1–14 Use A as CC.
Rows 15–42 Use B as CC, working rows 15–28, then rows 1–14 of pat.
Rows 43–56 Use A as CC, working rows 15–28 of pat.
Loosely bind off all sts purlwise. ■

Buttoned Capelet

This sweet capelet is knit in one strip from side to side, with the lace edge worked along with the body and shaped with short rows.

◆

Designed by Lisa Craig

SIZES
Adult woman

KNITTED MEASUREMENTS
Upper edge approx 34"/86.5cm
Length approx 9"/23cm

MATERIALS
■ Two 3½oz/100g skeins (each approx 220yd/201m) of Universal Yarn *Deluxe Worsted* (100% wool) in #12182 gold spice

■ One pair size 7 (4.5mm) needles OR SIZE TO OBTAIN GAUGE

■ Size 7 (4.5mm) crochet hook (for button loops)

■ 3 buttons

GAUGE
20 sts and 40 rows = 4"/10cm over garter st using size 7 (4.5mm) needles. TAKE TIME TO CHECK GAUGE.

SHORT ROW WRAP & TURN (W&T)
on RS row (on WS row)
1) Wyib (wyif), sl next st purlwise.
2) Move yarn between the needles to the front (back).
3) Sl the same st back to LH needle. Turn work. One st is wrapped.
4) When working the wrapped st, insert RH needle under the wrap and work it tog with the corresponding st on needle.

NOTE
The stitch count changes as the lace edging is worked.

CAPELET
Cast on 45 sts.
Row 1 (RS) K42, (yo) twice, k2tog, k1.
Row 2 (short row WS) K2, (k1, p1) in double yo, k5, p3, k31, w&t.
Row 3 (short row RS) K31, yo, SK2P, yo, k9.
Row 4 K9, p3, k34.
Row 5 K41, [(yo) twice, k2tog] twice, k1.
Row 6 (short row WS) K2, [(k1, p1) in double yo, k1] twice, k3, p3, k8, w&t.
Row 7 (short row RS) K8, yo, SK2P, yo, k11.
Row 8 K11, p3, k34.
Row 9 K41, [(yo) twice, k2tog] 3 times, k1.
Row 10 (short row WS) K2, [(k1, p1) in double yo, k1] 3 times, k3, p3, k31, w&t.
Row 11 (short row RS) K31, yo, SK2P, yo, k14.
Row 12 Bind off 6 sts, k until 8 sts on RH needle, p3, k34.
Rep rows 1–12 for 31 times more. Then, rep rows 1–11 once more. Bind off.

FINISHING
Sew buttons to edge of right front, using photo as guide. With crochet hook, ch 12 for each of 3 button loops. Tack chains at each end to left front edge to correspond to buttons. ■

Stripes & Columns Hat

Columns of twisted stitches add three-dimensionality and a bright pompom adds playfulness to a sporty striped hat.

Designed by Lori Steinberg

SIZE
Adult woman

KNITTED MEASUREMENTS
Brim circumference, unstretched
14"/35.5cm
Length, not including pompom
10"/25.5cm

MATERIALS
■ One 3½oz/100g skein (each approx 220yd/200m) of Universal Yarn *Deluxe Worsted* (100% wool) each in #13105 straw (A), #12182 gold spice (B), and #3608 marigold (C)

■ One pair size 8 (5mm) needles OR SIZE TO OBTAIN GAUGE

■ Stitch markers

GAUGE
16 sts and 29 rows = 4"/10cm over garter st using size 8 (5mm) needles.
TAKE TIME TO CHECK GAUGE.

STITCH GLOSSARY
2-st RT K2tog without dropping st from LH needle, k the first st again, letting both sts drop from LH needle.

STRIPE SEQUENCE
*2 rows B, 6 rows A, 2 rows C, 6 rows A, 2 rows B, 4 rows A; rep from * for stripe sequence.

NOTE
When working rows in colors B or C, slip the 2 sts in the 2-st RT column without working them.

BRIM
With A, cast on 10 sts. Knit 102 rows. Bind off.

HAT BODY
With A, *pick up and k 1 st, yo; rep from * evenly along side edge of brim until there are 96 sts on needle, pick up and k 2 sts—98 sts.
Set-up row (WS) K8, [p2, k14] 5 times, p2, k8.
Next (inc) row (RS) K8, [yo, 2-st RT, yo, k14] five times, yo, 2-st RT, yo, k8—110 sts.
Next row K9, [p2, k16] five times, p2, k to end.

Next row K9 [2-st RT, k16] 5 times, 2-st RT, k to end.
Rep last 2 rows for pat st and beg stripe sequence.
Cont in this manner until piece measures 5"/12.5cm from pick-up row, end with a WS row.

SHAPE CROWN
Next (dec) row (RS) [K to 2 sts before 2-st RT, k2tog, 2-st RT, k2tog] 6 times, k to end—12 sts dec'd.
Rep dec row every 4th row 3 times, then every other row 3 times more—26 sts.
Work 1 WS row.
Next (dec) row (RS) K1, [k2tog] 12 times, k1—14 sts
Next (dec) row (WS) K1 [k2tog] 6 times, k1—8 sts.
Break yarn, leaving a long tail. Thread tail through open sts twice, draw closed and secure.

FINISHING
Sew seam from top to lower edge, including brim.
With C, make a 2"/5cm pompom and sew to top of hat. ■

Mitered Squares Baby Blanket

This graphic blanket is constructed by sewing together 16 squares, each with blocks of 4 soft colors crisscrossed by white.

Designed by Stacey Gerbman

KNITTED MEASUREMENTS
38½ x 38½"/97.5 x 97.5cm

MATERIALS
■ Two 3½oz/100g skeins (each approx 220yd/201m) of Universal Yarn *Deluxe Worsted* (100% wool) each in #12502 smoke heather (A) and #12507 shamrock heather (C)

■ 1 skein each in #13105 straw (B), #13103 channel (D), and #13109 stone (E)

■ One each size 8 (5mm) circular needles, 16 and 40"/40 and 100cm long, OR SIZE TO OBTAIN GAUGE

■ Stitch markers

GAUGE
16 sts and 36 rows = 4"/10cm over garter st using size 8 (5mm) needles.
TAKE TIME TO CHECK GAUGE.

NOTE
Blanket is made up of 16 squares. Each square is worked with a center cross in color A, then mitered squares are picked up and knit in each corner in different colors.

CENTER CROSS
(make 16)
With shorter circular needle and A, cast on 12 sts.
Knit 23 rows.
Next row (RS) K12, cast on 12 sts— 24 sts.
Next row K24, cast on 12 sts—36 sts.
Knit 20 rows.
Next row (RS) Bind off 12 sts, k to end—24 sts.
Next row Bind off 12 sts, k to end— 36 sts.
Knit 23 rows. Bind off.

SQUARE 1
(make 8)
CORNER 1
With RS facing, shorter circular needle, and B, beg at left side of upper bound-off edge and pick up and k 12 sts along upper side edge, pick up and k 1 st at corner, pick up and k 12 sts along bound-off edge of center cross—25 sts. Place marker in center stitch and move this marker up every row.
Next row (WS) K to 1 st before marked stitch, SK2P, k to end— 2 sts dec'd.
Next row Knit.
Rep these 2 rows 10 times more—3 sts.
Next row SK2P. Fasten off.

CORNER 2
With RS facing, shorter circular needle, and C, beg at right side of bound-off edge of center cross and pick up and k 12 sts along bound-off edge, pick up and k 1 st at corner, pick up and k 12 sts along upper side edge—25 sts. Complete as for corner 1.

CORNER 3
With RS facing, shorter circular needle, and D, beg at left side of cast-on edge of center cross and pick up and k 12 sts along lower edge, pick up and k 1 st at corner, pick up and k 12 sts along lower side edge—25 sts. Complete as for corner 1.

CORNER 4
With RS facing, shorter circular needle, and E, beg at right side of cast-on edge of center cross and pick up and k 12 sts along side edge, pick up and k 1 st at corner, pick up and k 12 sts along lower edge of center cross—25 sts. Complete as for corner 1.

SQUARE 2
(make 8)
Work as for square 1, using E for corner 1, C for corner 2, D for corner 3, and B for corner 4.

FINISHING

With RS facing, arrange squares, alternating squares 1 and 2 using photo as guide, or in a pleasing arrangement. Sew squares tog.

BORDER

With RS facing, longer circular needle, and C, beg at top right corner, pick up and k 144 sts. Knit 6 rows. Bind off, leaving last loop on needle. Turn to work along right side edge of blanket. *Beg along side of border just worked, pick up and k 4 sts along edge of border, pick up and k 144 sts along edge of blanket—149 sts. Knit 6 rows. Bind off, leaving last loop on needle. Knit 6 rows. Bind off, leaving last loop on needle. Turn to work along next edge of blanket. Rep from * once more.

Beg along side of border just worked, pick up and k 4 sts along edge of border, pick up and k 144 sts along edge of blanket, pick up and k 5 sts along edge of first border worked. Knit 6 rows. Bind off. ∎

Nesting Bird

A mop-top birdie with embroidered features is happy to keep a little one company from the comfort of its knitted nest.

Designed by Pat Olski

KNITTED MEASUREMENTS
Circumference at widest point (stuffed)
15"/38cm
Length (stuffed) approx 9"/23cm

MATERIALS
■ One 3½oz/100g skein (each approx 220yd/201m) of Universal Yarn *Deluxe Worsted Superwash* (100% wool) each in #733 sweatshirt grey and #716 nitrox blue (B)

■ Small amounts of embroidery thread in gold (C) and black (D)

■ One pair size 6 (4mm) needles OR SIZE TO OBTAIN GAUGE

■ Tapestry needle

■ Stuffing

■ Removable stitch markers

GAUGE
20 sts and 27 rows = 4"/10cm over garter st using size 6 (4mm) needles.
TAKE TIME TO CHECK GAUGE.

NEST

With A, cast on 6 sts. Knit 1 row.
Inc row 1 (RS) *K1, kfb; rep from *
to end—9 sts.
Inc row 2 *K1, kfb; rep from *
across, k1.
Rep inc row 2 once more—19 sts.
Knit 1 row.
Rep inc row 2 once—28 sts.
Knit 2 rows.
Rep inc row 1 once—42 sts.
Knit 3 rows.
Next (inc) row (WS) *K1, kfb; rep
from * across, k2—60 sts.
Place a marker in the end of this row.
Work even until piece measures 4¾"/12cm
from marker, end with a WS row.
Rep inc row 1 once more—90 sts.
Knit 1 row. Bind off. Break A.

BEGIN BIRD

Fold bound-off edge 1"/2.5cm to RS. With
A, pick up and k 60 sts in back of sts in
folded row. Change to B.
Knit 16 rows.

SHAPE BIRD HEAD

Next (dec) row (RS) K2, [k2tog, k7]
6 times, k2tog, k2—53 sts.
Knit 3 rows.
Next (dec) row (RS) K2, [k2tog, k6]
6 times, k2tog, k1—46 sts.
Knit 3 rows.
Next (dec) row (RS) K5, [K2tog, k5]
5 times, k2tog, k4—40 sts.
Knit 3 rows.
Next (dec) row (RS) K4, [k2tog, k4]
6 times—34 sts.
Knit 3 rows.
Next (dec) row (RS) K3, [k2tog, k3]
6 times, k1—28 sts.
Knit 3 rows.

Next (dec) row (RS) K2, [k2tog, k2]
6 times, k2—22 sts.
Knit 3 rows.
Next (dec) row (RS) K2, [k2tog, k1]
6 times, k2—16 sts.
Break yarn, leaving a long tail. Thread tail
through open sts to close.

WINGS

(make 2)
With A, cast on 18 sts. Knit 1 row.
Next (dec) row (RS) K to last 2 sts,
k2tog—1 st dec'd.
Next row Sl 1, k to end.
Rep last 2 rows 8 times more—9 sts.
Bind off.

BEAK

With C, cast on 5 sts.
Knit 1 row.
Next (dec) row (RS) SKP, k1,
K2tog—3 sts.
Next row SK2P. Fasten off.

FINISHING

With D and tapestry needle, make 2
French knots for eyes, using photo as
guide for placement. Center beak between
eyes and sew in place. Sew wings in place,
using photo as guide.
Sew back seam, leaving a small opening
for stuffing. Stuff toy and sew closed.

TOP FEATHERS

With B, wrap yarn around fingers
15 times. Attach a piece of yarn to top
of head and anchor loops firmly to top.
Cut loops. ■

Textured Lace Scarf

This gorgeous but deceptively easy-to-knit scarf features an allover lace pattern with borders worked separately and sewn on at each end.

◆

Designed by Linda Medina

◼◼◻◻

KNITTED MEASUREMENTS
7 x 58"/18 x 147cm

MATERIALS
■ Two 3½oz/100g skeins (each approx 220yd/201m) of Universal Yarn *Deluxe Worsted* (100% wool) in #91467 tulipwood

■ One pair size 9 (5.5mm) needles OR SIZE TO OBTAIN GAUGE

GAUGE
19 sts and 22 rows = 4"/10cm over pattern st using size 9 (5.5mm) needles. TAKE TIME TO CHECK GAUGE.

PATTERN STITCH
(multiple of 6 sts plus 3)
Row 1 and all WS rows Knit.
Row 2 K2, *yo, ssk, k1, k2tog, yo, k1; rep from * to last st, k1.
Row 4 K2, *yo, k1, SK2P, k1, yo, k1; rep from * to last st, k1.
Row 6 K2, *k2tog, yo, k1, yo, ssk, k1; rep from * to last st, k1.
Row 8 K1, k2tog, *[k1, yo] twice, k1, SK2P; rep from * to last 6 sts, [k1, yo] twice, k1, ssk, k1.
Rep rows 1–8 for pat st.

NOTE
Borders are knit separately and sewn to ends in finishing.

SCARF
Cast on 33 sts. Work rows 1–8 of stitch pattern 40 times. Knit 1 row. Bind off.

BORDER
(make 2)
Note Count sts after row 1 or row 12. If you knit loosely, go down 1 needle size for edging.
Cast on 9 sts.
Row 1 and all RS rows Knit.
Row 2 K3, k2tog, yo, k2tog, [yo, k1] twice.
Row 4 K2, [k2tog, yo] twice, k3, yo, k1.
Row 6 K1, [k2tog, yo] twice, k5, yo, k1.
Row 8 K3, [yo, k2tog] twice, k1, k2tog, yo, k2tog.
Row 10 K4, yo, k2tog, yo, k3tog, yo, k2tog.
Row 12 K5, yo, k3tog, yo, k2tog.
Rep rows 1–12 four times more. Bind off, leaving long tail for sewing.

FINISHING
Block scarf and edgings to measurements. With tail, whipstitch borders to each end of scarf. ■

Contrast Band Capelet

The multidirectional lines of garter stitch are enough to provide structure and visual interest in a capelet shaped with increases and short rows.

Designed by Kathy North

SIZE
Adult woman

KNITTED MEASUREMENTS
Width at upper edge, not including ties 20"/51cm

MATERIALS
■ Two 3½oz/100g skeins (each approx 220yd/201m) of Universal Yarn *Deluxe Worsted* (100% wool) in #12235 sidewalk grey (MC)

■ One skein in #12273 plum dandy (CC)

■ Size 10 (6mm) circular needle, 29"/74cm long, OR SIZE TO OBTAIN GAUGE

■ Size 8 (5mm) circular needle, 24"/60cm long

■ One set (5) size 8 (5mm) double-pointed needles (dpns)

GAUGE
16 sts and 31 rows = 4"/10cm over garter st using larger needle.
TAKE TIME TO CHECK GAUGE.

CABLE CAST-ON
1) Make a slip knot on LH needle. Insert RH needle knitwise, wrap yarn around needle as if to knit.
2) Draw the yarn through the stitch to make a new stitch, but do not drop the old stitch from the LH needle.
3) Slip the new stitch to the LH needle.
4) Insert RH needle between the first 2 sts on the needle. Wrap yarn around needle as if to knit and draw the yarn through to make a new stitch.
5) Slip the new stitch to the LH needle. Rep steps 4 and 5 until the number of sts required has been cast on.

NOTE
Capelet is worked in back and forth in rows. Circular needle is used to accommodate large number of sts. Do not join.

CAPELET
YOKE
With MC and larger needle, cast on 20 sts loosely.
Knit 6 rows.
Next (inc) row (RS) K2, M1, k to last 2 sts, M1, k2—2 sts inc'd.
Cont in garter st (k every row), rep inc row every 4th row twice more—26 sts.
Knit 3 rows.
Next (eyelet) row (RS) K2, *yo, k1; rep from * to last 2 sts, yo, k2—49 sts.
Knit 4 rows.

Next (inc) row (WS) K24, M1, k to end—50 sts.
Next (eyelet) row (RS) K2, *yo, k2; rep from * to last 2 sts, yo, k2—74 sts.
Knit 4 rows.
Next (inc) row (WS) K36, M1, k2, M1, k to end—76 sts.
Next (eyelet) row (RS) K2, *yo, k3; rep from * to last 2 sts, yo, k2—101 sts.
Knit 4 rows.
Next (dec) row (WS) K50, k2tog, k to end—100 sts.
Next (eyelet) row (RS) K2, *yo, k4; rep from * to last 2 sts, yo, k2—125 sts.
Knit 4 rows.
Next (dec) row (WS) K62, k2tog, k to end—124 sts.
Next (inc) row (RS) K2, *M1, k6; rep from * to end, M1, k2—145 sts.
Knit 5 rows.

BEGIN BODY OF CAPELET
Using cable cast-on method, cast on 37 sts at beg of row—182 sts.
Next row (RS) K36, k2tog (last cast-on st with 1 st from yoke), turn, k37.
Next row (RS) Sl 1 knitwise, k35, k2tog, turn, k37.
Rep last row until all sts from yoke have been worked. Break MC.

RIGHT FRONT BAND
Next row (RS) With CC, k37, pick up and k 5 sts along edge of yoke to first eyelet row, turn—42 sts.
Knit 5 rows. Bind off loosely.

LEFT FRONT BAND

With RS facing, larger needle, and CC, beg at last eyelet row, pick up and k 42 sts along edge of capelet to lower edge. Knit 5 rows. Bind off loosely.

NECKBAND

With smaller needle, CC and RS facing, beg at right front band, pick up and k 78 sts evenly along upper edge of capelet, including left front band. Knit 1 row. Break yarn and set work aside.

TIES

With dpn and CC, cast on 8 sts.
Next row (RS) Sl 1 knitwise, k7.
Cont in garter st, slipping first st of every row knitwise, until piece measures 8"/12.5cm from beg, end with a WS row.

JOIN TIE TO CAPELET

Place sts from dpn on LH end of smaller circular needle.
Next row (RS) Sl 1 knitwise, k6, k2tog (last tie st, with 1 st from neck), turn, k to end.
Rep last row until all neckband sts have been joined. Place a marker at end of last row.
Next row (RS) Sl 1 knitwise, k7.
Rep last row until tie measures 8"/12.5cm from marker. Bind off. ∎

Lacy Heart Shawl

Garter stitch and lace balance each other perfectly in a sweet triangular shawl with a pattern that subtly evokes heart shapes.

Designed by Lois S. Young

KNITTED MEASUREMENTS
Width (after blocking) 62"/157.5cm
Depth at center point 30"/76cm

MATERIALS
▪ Three 3½oz/100g skeins (each approx 220yd/201m) of Universal Yarn *Deluxe Worsted* (100% wool) in #14005 orchid

▪ One size 9 (5.5mm) circular needle, 40"/100cm long, OR SIZE TO OBTAIN GAUGE

GAUGE
13 sts and 27 rows = 4"/10cm over chart pat using size 9 (5.5mm) needle. TAKE TIME TO CHECK GAUGE.

NOTES
1) Bind off very loosely, pulling extra slack into sts as they are passed over, or bind off with a needle one size larger.
2) When adding a new ball of yarn, add it at the beginning of row and work first k st with both working yarn and new yarn, then drop working yarn and cont with new yarn.

STITCH GLOSSARY

M1R Insert LH needle from back to front under the strand between last st worked and next st on LH needle. K into the front loop to twist the st.

M1L Insert LH needle from front to back under the strand between last st worked and next st on LH needle. K into the back loop to twist the st.

SHAWL

Loosely cast on 2 sts. Knit 1 row.
Row 1 (RS) Sl 1, M1R, k1tbl—3 sts.
Rows 2 and 4 Sl 1, k to last st, k1tbl.
Rows 3 and 5 Sl 1, M1R, k to last st, M1L, k1tbl—2 sts inc'd.
Row 6 Rep row 2—7 sts.

BEGIN CHART 1

Work rows 1–12 of chart 1—19 sts.

BEGIN CHART 2

Row 1 (RS) Work to rep line, work 6-st rep, work to end of chart.
Cont to work chart in this manner until row 12 is complete.
Rep rows 1–12 for 14 times more, working 6-st rep 2 additional times across each time the 12 rows are complete.
Next row (RS) Sl 1, k to end.
Bind off loosely knitwise (see note above).

Block firmly, pinning to full size on blocking board. Mist with water and allow to dry. ∎

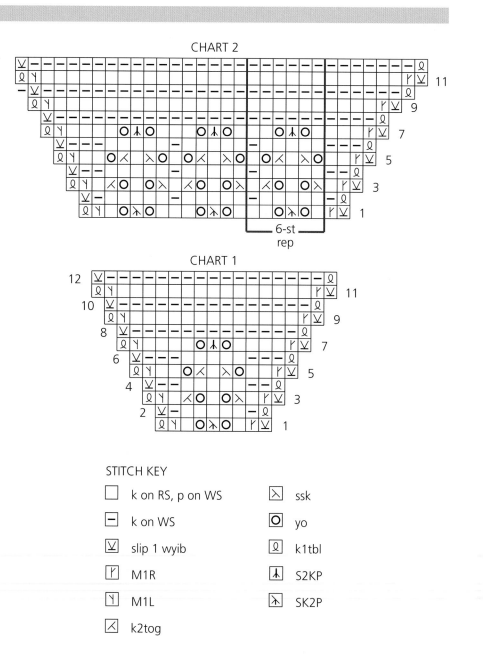

CHART 2

6-st rep

CHART 1

STITCH KEY

☐	k on RS, p on WS	⋋	ssk
–	k on WS	O	yo
Ⅴ	slip 1 wyib	Ω	k1tbl
Ր	M1R	⅄	S2KP
Ⴗ	M1L	⅄	SK2P
⋌	k2tog		

Unisex Striped Hat

What could be simpler—and more classic—than a striped beanie?
Add pizzazz to the woman's version with a handy premade pompom.

◆

Designed by Carol J. Sulcoski

◼◼◻◻◻

SIZES
Adult woman (adult man)

KNITTED MEASUREMENTS
Brim circumference (unstretched)
20 (22)"/51 (56)cm
Length 8"/20.5cm

MATERIALS
Woman's hat
◼ One 3½oz/100g skein (each approx 220yd/201m) of Universal Yarn *Deluxe Worsted* (100% wool) each in #12294 real red (A) and #12236 violet glow (B)

Man's hat
◼ One 3½oz/100g skein (each approx 220yd/201m) of Universal Yarn *Deluxe Worsted* (100% wool) each in #3677 cobalt (A) and #12279 blue lagoon (B)

◼ Size 9 (5.5mm) circular needle, 16"/40cm long, OR SIZE TO OBTAIN GAUGE

◼ One set (5) size 9 (5.5mm) double-pointed needles (dpns)

◼ Stitch marker

For woman's hat only
◼ Universal Yarns Luxury Fur Pom-Pom in #103-07 purple

GAUGE
16 sts and 28 rows = 4"/10cm over garter st using size 9 (5.5mm) needle.
TAKE TIME TO CHECK GAUGE.

HAT
With circular needle and A, cast on 80 (88) sts. Join, taking care not to twist sts, and place marker (pm) for beg of rnd. Work 10 (12) rnds in garter st (knit 1 rnd, purl 1 rnd).
With B, work 2 rnds.
With A, work 7 (9) rnds.
With B, work 2 rnds.
With A, work 7 rnds.
With B, work 2 rnds.
With A, work 14 (10) rnds.

SHAPE CROWN
Note Change to dpns when sts no longer fit comfortably on circular needle.

For woman's hat only
Rnd 1 [K8, k2tog] 8 times—72 sts. Work 3 rnds even in pat.
Rnd 5 [K7, k2tog] 8 times—64 sts. Work 3 rnds.
Rnd 9 [K6, k2tog] 8 times—56 sts. Work 3 rnds.
Rnd 13 [K5, k2tog] 8 times—48 sts. Work 1 rnd. Break A and work to end in B.

For man's hat only
Rnd 1 [K9, k2tog] 8 times—80 sts. Work 1 rnd even in pat.
Rnd 3 [K8, k2tog] 8 times—72 sts. Work 1 rnd.
Rnd 5 [K7, k2tog] 8 times—64 sts. Work 1 rnd. Break A and work to end in B.
Rnd 7 [K6, k2tog] 8 times—56 sts. Work 1 rnd.
Rnd 9 [K5, k2tog] 8 times—48 sts. Work 1 rnd.

For both sizes
Next rnd [K4, k2tog] 8 times—40 sts. Work 1 rnd.
Next rnd [K3, k2tog] 8 times—32 sts. Work 1 rnd.
Next rnd [K2, k2tog] 8 times—24 sts. Work 1 rnd.
Next rnd [K1, k2tog] 8 times—16 sts. Work 1 rnd.
Next rnd [K2tog] 8 times—8 sts. Work 1 rnd.
Break yarn and draw through rem sts. For woman's hat, attach pompom to top of hat. ◼

Lace-Edge Shawlette

A wrap with modern stripes and short-row shaping gets a dose
of distinctly feminine flair from a wide lace edging.

Designed by Cheryl Murray

KNITTED MEASUREMENTS
Width at lower edge approx
68"/172.5cm
Depth at center 12"/30.5cm

MATERIALS
■ One 3½oz/100g skein (each approx
220yd/201m) of Universal Yarn
Deluxe Worsted (100% wool) each in
#71051 toast (A), #12189 baby blue
(B), and #12299 chocolate (C)

■ Size 8 (5mm) circular needle,
32"/80cm long, OR SIZE TO OBTAIN
GAUGE

GAUGE
16 sts and 40 rows = 4"/10cm over
garter st using size 8 (5mm) needles.
TAKE TIME TO CHECK GAUGE.

SHORT ROW WRAP & TURN
(W&T)
on RS row (on WS row)
1) Wyib (wyif), sl next st purlwise.
2) Move yarn between the needles to
the front (back).
3) Sl the same st back to LH needle.
Turn work. One st is wrapped.
4) It is not necessary to pick up the
wraps when working short rows in
garter st.

EDGING
With A, cast on 20 sts.
Work rows 1–8 of chart 48 times.
Bind off.

SHAWL
With RS facing and B, pick up and k 192
sts along straight side edge of edging,
working into the front leg of every sl st.

BEGIN SHORT ROW SEQUENCE
*****Short row 1** K112, w&t.
Short row 2 K32, w&t.
Short row 3 K to 16 sts past last
wrapped st, w&t.
Rep short row 3 until all sts have been
worked.* Break B and join C.

With C, k 1 row. With C, rep from * to *.
With A, k 2 rows over all sts.
With B, rep from * to *.
With A, k 2 rows over all sts.
With C, rep from * to *.
With B, rep from * to *. With B, bind off
loosely.

FINISHING
Block lightly to measurements. ■

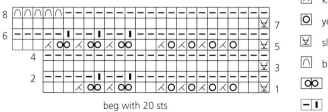

beg with 20 sts

STITCH KEY
☐ k on RS
➖ k on WS
☒ k2tog
Ⓞ yo
⤓ slip 1 wyif
⌒ bind off
⧄⧄ yo twice
➖▮ (k1, p1) into double yo

48

Starlight Stole

Simple garter stitch bands in two colors reach glamorous heights when one is a silvery metallic made to catch the light.

Designed by Galina Carroll

KNITTED MEASUREMENTS
Approx 20 x 72"/51 x 182.5cm

MATERIALS
■ Three 3½oz/100g skeins (each approx 220yd/201m) of Universal Yarn *Deluxe Worsted* (100% wool) in #12270 natural (A)

■ Two .88oz/25g skeins (each approx 200yd/183m) of Universal Yarn *Cotton Gold* (cotton/payette/metallic) in #1098 silver (B)

■ One pair size 8 (5.5mm) needles OR SIZE TO OBTAIN GAUGE

GAUGE
15 sts and 20 rows = 4"/10cm over garter st using size 8 (5mm) needles and A.
TAKE TIME TO CHECK GAUGE.

NOTES
1) Once the first 6 rows of stripe pat are complete, join a 2nd ball of A to rib the last 5 sts of every row. Do not carry A across the WS of work.
2) Carry yarn not used up the side of work.
3) When changing colors, twist yarns to prevent holes.

STOLE
With A, cast on 76 sts.
Next row (RS) *K1, p1; rep from * to last st, k1.
Next row (WS) K the knit sts and p the purl sts as they appear.
Rep last row for k1, p1 rib until 10 rows are complete.

BEGIN STRIPE PAT
Rows 1–6 With A, rib 5 sts, k to last 5 sts, rib 5 sts.
Rows 7–9 With A, rib 5 sts, with B, k to last 5 sts, with 2nd ball of A, rib 5 sts.
Rows 10–15 Picking up each ball of A when you come to it, rib 5 sts, k to last 5 sts, rib 5 sts.
Rep rows 7–15 for 36 times more—37 bands of B have been worked. Break B.
Rep rows 1–6 once more.
With A, work 10 rows in k1, p1 rib.
Bind off.

FRINGE
*Cut 2 strands of A, each 13"/33cm long. Holding both strands tog, fold in half, forming a loop. With crochet hook, draw the loop though 1 st on cast-on edge of stole. Pull the ends of the strands through the loop and pull to tighten. Rep from * 18 times evenly along cast-on edge. Rep for bound-off edge. ■

Double Stitch Cowl

Double the stitch patterns, double the personality: the garter stitch and lace halves of this long cowl are joined at the ends using 3-needle bind-off.

Designed by Sandi Prosser

KNITTED MEASUREMENTS
Circumference 58"/147.5cm
Width 7"/18cm

MATERIALS
■ One 3½oz/100g skein (each approx 220yd/201m) of Universal Yarn *Deluxe Worsted* (100% wool) each in #3620 coral (A) and #91468 sunkissed coral (B)

■ One pair each sizes 6 and 7 (4 and 4.5mm) needles OR SIZE TO OBTAIN GAUGE

■ Size G/6 (4mm) crochet hook and scrap yarn for provisional cast-on

GAUGES
23 sts and 40 rows = 4"/10cm over garter st using size 6 (4mm) needles.
24 sts and 31 rows = 4"/10cm in lace pat using size 7 (4.5mm) needles.
TAKE TIME TO CHECK GAUGES.

PROVISIONAL CAST-ON
With scrap yarn and crochet hook, ch the number of sts to cast on plus a few extra. Cut a tail and pull the tail through the last chain. With knitting needle and yarn, pick up and knit the stated number of sts through the "purl bumps" on the back of the chain.

To remove scrap yarn chain, when instructed, pull out the tail from the last crochet stitch. Gently and slowly pull on the tail to unravel the crochet stitches, carefully placing each released knit stitch on a needle.

3-NEEDLE BIND-OFF
1) Hold right sides of pieces together on 2 needles. Insert 3rd needle knitwise into first st of each needle, and wrap yarn knitwise.
2) Knit these 2 sts together, and slip them off the needles. *Knit the next 2 sts together in the same manner.
3) Slip first st on 3rd needle over 2nd st and off needle. Rep from * in step 2 across row until all sts are bound off.

STITCH GLOSSARY
RT (right twist) K2tog and leave on LH needle, k first st again, sl both sts from LH needle.
LT (left twist) With RH needle behind LH needle, skip first st and k the 2nd st tbl, then knit both sts tog tbl.

LACE PATTERN
(multiple of 4 sts)
Row 1 (WS) *K1, p2, k1; rep from * to end.
Row 2 *K2tog, [yo] twice, ssk; rep from * to end.
Row 3 *P1, [k1, p1] into double yo, p1; rep from * to end.
Row 4 K1, *p2, RT; rep from * to last 3 sts, p2, k1.
Row 5 *P1, k2, p1; rep from * to end.
Row 6 Yo, *ssk, k2tog, [yo twice]; rep from * to last 4 sts, ssk, k2tog, yo.
Row 7 K1, *p2, [k1, p1] into double yo; rep from * to last 3 sts, p2, k1.
Row 8 *P1, LT, p1; rep from * to end.
Rep rows 1–8 for lace pat.

COWL
With smaller needles and A, cast on 40 sts using provisional cast-on. Work in garter st (k every row) until piece measures 29"/73.5cm from beg, end with a WS row. Break A and join B.
Next row (RS) With A, knit, inc 2 sts evenly across—42 sts.
Change to larger needles and beg lace pat as foll:
Row 1 (WS) K3, work lace pat over 36 sts, k3.
Cont to work lace pat in this way, working 3 sts at each edge in garter st, until piece measures 58"/147.5cm from beg, end with a WS row.
Next row (RS) Knit, dec 2 sts evenly across—40 sts.

FINISHING
Remove scrap yarn from provisional cast-on and place sts on needle. Join ends using 3-needle bind-off.
Block lightly to measurements. ■

Asymmetric Striped Shawl

The sawtooth edge of this top-down shawl evokes a collegiate banner—knit it in your school colors!

◆

Designed by Dana Elizabeth Freed

◀■■■▭

KNITTED MEASUREMENTS
Length from back neck to point of edging 12½"/31.5cm
Width at lower edge approx 85¾"/217.5cm

MATERIALS
■ Two 3½oz/100g skeins (each approx 220yd/201m) of Universal Yarn *Deluxe Worsted* (100% wool) each in #3677 cobalt (A) and #12502 smoke heather (B)

■ Size 9 (5.5mm) circular needle, 40"/100cm long, OR SIZE TO OBTAIN GAUGE

■ Stitch markers

GAUGE
14 sts and 30 rows = 4"/10cm over garter st using size 9 (5.5mm) needles.
TAKE TIME TO CHECK GAUGE.

NOTE
Shawl is worked back and forth in rows. Circular needle is used to accommodate large number of sts. Do not join.

SHAWL
With A, cast on 3 sts, place marker (pm), cast on 3 sts more, pm, cast on 50 sts more—56 sts.
Inc row 1 (RS) K1, kfb, k to marker, sl marker, kfb, k to 1 st before next marker, kfb, sl marker—4 sts inc'd.
Inc row 2 (WS) K1, kfb, k to last 2 sts, kfb, k1—2 sts inc'd.
Rep inc rows 1 and 2, working in color sequence as foll: 8 rows more in A, 2 rows B, 2 rows A, 2 rows B, 6 rows A, 2 rows B, 2 rows A, 2 rows B, 10 rows A, 10 rows B, 2 rows A, 2 rows B, 2 rows A, 6 rows B, 2 rows A, 2 rows B, 2 rows A, 10 rows B, 2 rows A, 2 rows B—296 sts.
Break B.
With A, rep inc row 1—300 sts.

BEGIN EDGING
*Row 1 (WS) With WS facing, k1, turn.
Row 2 (RS) K1, turn.
Rows 3 and 4 K2, turn.
Rows 4 and 5 K3, turn.
Rows 6 and 7 K4, turn,
Cont in this manner, working 1 st more in each WS row, until RS row *K10, turn* has been worked. Bind off 10 sts.
Rep from * until all sts have been incorporated into edging. Fasten off. ■

Mosaic Rectangles Scarf

The graphic colorwork pattern on this unisex scarf is knit in the mosaic style, with only one color used per row.

Designed by Cheryl Murray

◀■■■▭

KNITTED MEASUREMENTS
Approx 6 x 70"/15 x 177.5cm

MATERIALS
■ Two 3½oz/100g skeins (each approx 220yd/201m) of Universal Yarn *Deluxe Worsted* (100% wool) in #12278 mallard (A)

■ One skein in #12506 azure heather (B)

■ Size 7 (4.5mm) circular needle, 40"/100cm long, OR SIZE TO OBTAIN GAUGE

GAUGE
19 sts and 36 rows = 4"/10cm over chart pat using size 7 (4.5mm) needles.
TAKE TIME TO CHECK GAUGE.

NOTES
1) Scarf is worked lengthwise. Circular needle is used to accommodate large number of sts. Do not join.
2) This is a mosaic pattern. Only 1 color is used in each 2-row stripe; the color changes within the rows are created by slipping stitches as charted.

SCARF
With A, cast on 339 sts.

BEGIN CHART
Row 1 Work to rep line, work 12-st rep 28 times across, work to end of chart. Cont to work chart in this way until row 24 is complete. Rep rows 1–24 once more, then work rows 1–12 once more.
With A, knit 3 rows. Bind off loosely knitwise.

Block lightly to measurements. ■

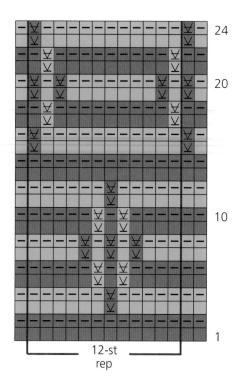

COLOR AND STITCH KEY
☐ k on RS

⊟ k on WS

� sl 1 wyif

⊻ sl 1 wyib

■ A

■ B

A Special Gift
for a Special
Friend

Lacy Poncho

Staggered blocks of lace and garter stitch form an eye-catching allover pattern that combines lightness and structure.

Designed by Sandi Prosser

SIZES
X-Small/Small/Medium and
Large/X-Large
Shown in size X-Small/Small/Medium

KNITTED MEASUREMENTS
Lower edge circumference 40½
(43¾)"/102.5 (111)cm
Length 11"/28cm

MATERIALS
■ Two 3½oz/100g skeins (each
approx 220yd/201m) of Universal
Yarn *Deluxe Worsted* (100% wool)
in #12144 starfish

■ One each sizes 6 and 7 (4 and
4.5mm) circular needles, 24"/60cm
long, OR SIZE TO OBTAIN GAUGE

■ Stitch marker

GAUGE
19 sts and 34 rnds = 4"/10cm over pat
st using larger needle.
TAKE TIME TO CHECK GAUGE.

GARTER LACE PATTERN
(multiple of 16 sts)
Rnds 1, 3, 5, and 7 *[Ssk, yo] twice,
k8, [ssk, yo] twice; rep from * around.
Rnds 2, 4, 6, and 8 *K4, p9, k3; rep
from * around.
Rnds 9, 11, 13, and 15 *K5, [yo,
k2tog] 4 times, k3; rep from * to around.
Rnds 10, 12, 14, and 16 *P5, k7,
p4; rep from * around.
Rep rnds 1–16 for garter lace pat.

PONCHO
With larger needle, cast on 192 (208) sts.
Join, being careful not to twist sts, and
place marker for beg of rnd. Purl 1 rnd.
Rnd 1 Work 16-st rep of garter lace pat
12 (13) times around.
Cont to work in this manner until rnd 16
is complete. Rep rnds 1–16 four times
more, then rnds 1–8 once.

NECK EDGING
Change to smaller needle.
Next (dec) rnd *K6, k2tog; rep from *
around—168 (182) sts.
Purl 1 rnd. Work 4 rnds more in garter st
(k 1 rnd, p 1 rnd).
Bind off purlwise.

Square Baby Cap & Cuffed Booties

Need a last-minute baby gift? This charming hat is formed from a basic rectangle with I-cord ties and a pompom echoed on the matching booties.

Designed by Lisa Craig

BABY CAP

SIZES
Newborn–3 months (6 months)
Shown in size 6 months

KNITTED MEASUREMENTS
Width from front edge to front edge
12½ (14½)"/31.5 (36.5)cm
Length 6¼ (7¼)"/16 (18.5)cm

MATERIALS
■ One 3½oz/100g skein (each approx 220yd/201m) of Universal Yarn *Deluxe Worsted Superwash* (100% wool) in #749 smoke heather (MC) *or* #748 oatmeal heather (MC)

■ Small amount in #718 dusty blue (CC) *or* #713 honey dew (CC)

■ One pair size 7 (4.5mm) needles OR SIZE TO OBTAIN GAUGE

■ One set (2) size 6 (4mm) double-pointed needles (dpns)

GAUGE
21 sts and 40 rows = 4"/10cm over garter st using size 7 (4.5mm) needles.
TAKE TIME TO CHECK GAUGE.

I-CORD
With 2 dpns, cast on 2 sts. *Knit one row. Without turning work, slide the sts back to the opposite end of needle to work next row from RS. Pull yarn tightly from the end of the row. Rep from * until cord measures desired length.

NOTE
The yarn amounts listed are enough to make both the cap and the matching booties.

CAP
With MC, cast on 66 (76) sts. Work in garter st (k every row) until piece measures 4½ (5½)"/11.5 (14)cm from beg. Bind off.

FINISHING
Fold piece in half and sew bound-off edge tog.
With CC, make a 1"/2.5cm pompom and sew to corner point of cap.

I-CORD TIES
(make 2)
With CC and dpn, cast on 2 sts. Work I-cord for 9"/23cm. K2tog and fasten off. Sew to corner of cap. Tie a knot at end of each cord. ■

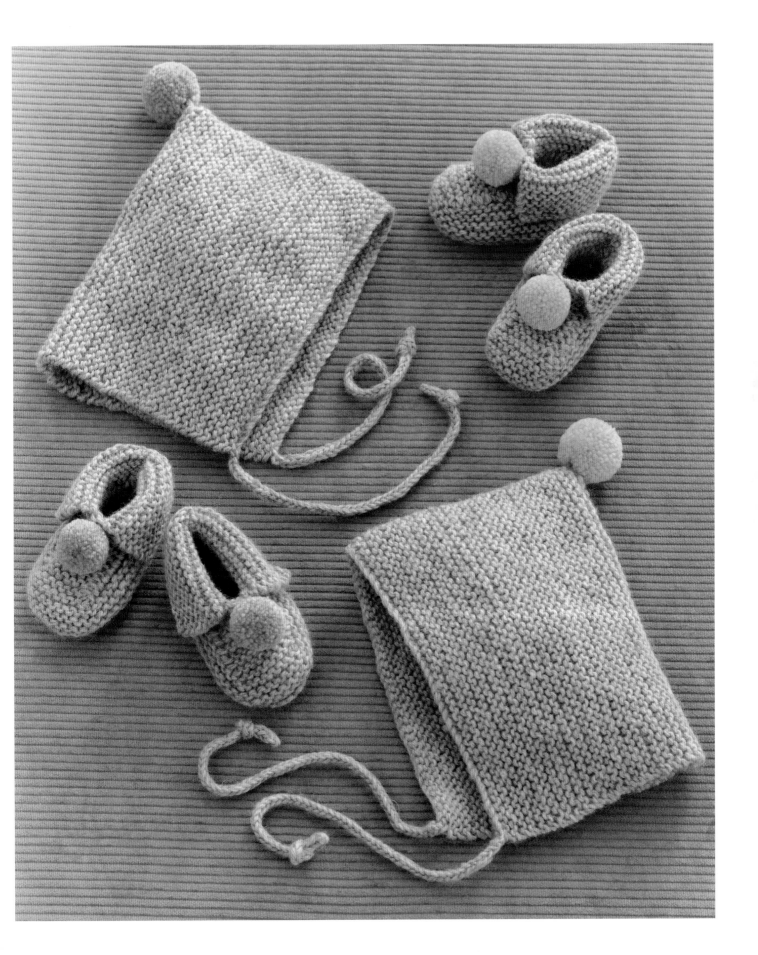

CUFFED BOOTIES

■■■□

SIZE
6 months

KNITTED MEASUREMENTS
Foot circumference approx 4"/10cm
Length 4"/10cm

MATERIALS
■ One 3½oz/100g skein (each approx 220yd/201m) of Universal Yarn *Deluxe Worsted Superwash* (100% wool) in #749 smoke heather (MC) *or* #748 oatmeal heather (MC)

■ Small amount in #718 dusty blue (CC) *or* #713 honey dew (CC)

■ One pair each sizes 3 and 6 (3.25 and 4mm) needles OR SIZE TO OBTAIN GAUGE

GAUGE
22 sts and 48 rows = 4"/10cm over garter st using larger needles.
TAKE TIME TO CHECK GAUGE.

NOTE
The yarn amounts listed will make both the booties and the matching cap.

BOOTIE
With MC, cast on 31 sts.
Row 1 and all WS rows Knit.
Row 2 (inc) K1, [M1, k14, M1, k1] twice—35 sts.
Row 4 (inc) K1, [M1, k16, M1, k1] twice—39 sts.

Row 6 (inc) K1, [M1, k18, M1, k1] twice—43 sts.
Row 8 (inc) K1, [M1, k20, M1, k1] twice—47 sts.
Knit 7 rows.

SHAPE INSTEP
Short row 1 (RS) K27, SKP, turn.
Short row 2 Sl 1, k7, k2tog, turn.
Short row 3 Sl 1, k7, SKP, turn.
Rep short rows 2 and 3 seven times more, then short row 2 once—29 sts rem.
Next row (RS) Knit to end of row. Change to smaller needles.
Next row Knit.
Next (rib) row [K1, p1] 5 times, k9, [p1, k1] 5 times.
Work in rib as established, working center 9 sts in St st for 3 rows more.
Next row (RS) Knit. Change to larger needles.

CUFF
Next row (WS) Knit.
Next row K14, turn, leaving rem sts on hold.
Cont on these 14 sts in garter st for 13 rows more. Bind off.
Rejoin yarn to rem sts, k2tog, k to end of row—14 sts.
Work 13 rows more in garter st. Bind off.

FINISHING
Sew sole and back-of-foot seam. Fold cuff to RS. With CC, make a ¾"/2cm pompom and sew to top of bootie, using photo as guide. ■

Drop Stitch Serape

An easy drop stitch pattern creates an allover mesh striped effect on this dramatic wrap for all seasons.

Designed by Kim Haesemeyer

KNITTED MEASUREMENTS
Width across back 31"/78.5cm
Length from back neck to
lower edge 30"/76cm

MATERIALS
■ Six 3½oz/100g skeins
(each approx 220yd/201m) of Universal
Yarn *Deluxe Worsted* (100% wool) in
#14006 raspberry

■ Size 6 (4mm) circular needle,
32"/80cm long, OR SIZE TO
OBTAIN GAUGE

■ Size G/6 (4mm) crochet hook

GAUGE
18 sts and 24 rows = 4"/10cm over
drop st pat using size 6 (4mm) needles.
TAKE TIME TO CHECK GAUGE.

DROP STITCH PATTERN
Rows 1–4 Knit.
Row 5 (RS) Knit, wrapping yarn
twice around needle for each st.
Row 6 Knit, dropping extra wraps.
Rep rows 1–6 for drop st pat.

NOTE
Piece is worked from side to side.

WRAP
Cast on 270 sts. Knit 1 (WS) row.

BEGIN DROP ST PAT
Rep rows 1–6 of drop st pat until
piece measures 13"/33cm from beg, end
with a row 4.

SHAPE NECK
Next row (RS) Bind off 135 sts, work
row 5 of pat to end.
Work even in pat as established on rem
135 sts for 5"/12.5cm, end with a row 6.
Cast on 135 sts at beg of next row.
Work even in pat as established until piece
measures 13"/33cm from neck cast-on,
end with a row 4. Bind off loosely.

FINISHING
Block to measurements. When piece is dry,
with crochet hook, work 1 row sc around
entire edge of wrap. ■

Pop of Color Accessories Bag

This lined drawstring pouch is a petite version of the Pop of Color Project Bag (page 69). Use it to hold smaller projects or needles and notions!

Designed by Jeannie Chin

KNITTED MEASUREMENTS
6¾ x 5 x 5"/17 x 12.5 x 12.5cm

MATERIALS
■ One 3½oz/100g skein (each approx 220yd/201m) of Universal Yarn *Deluxe Worsted* (100% wool) each in #1900 ebony (A), #12270 natural (B), and #3691 Christmas red (C)

■ One pair each sizes 4 and 6 (3.5 and 4mm) needles OR SIZE TO OBTAIN GAUGE

■ ¾yd/.75m black cotton fabric

■ ⅛yd/.125m black lightweight interfacing for eyelets

■ Sewing needle and black thread

■ Note that if you are making the project bag, no additional materials are needed for the accessories bag

GAUGE
20 sts and 44 rows = 4"/10cm over garter st using larger needles.
TAKE TIME TO CHECK GAUGE.

STITCH GLOSSARY
MB (make bobble) (K1, yo, k1) in same st, turn, k3, turn, p3, turn, k3, turn, S2KP.
LS (long st) Insert RH needle through purl loop 2 rows below and knit it tog with next st on needle.

PATTERN STITCH
(multiple of 6 sts plus 1)
Rows 1 and 2 With A, knit.
Row 3 With B, knit.
Row 4 (RS) With B, *k1, LS; rep from * to last st, k1.
Rows 5 and 6 With A, knit.
Rows 7 and 8 With B, knit.
Rows 9–12 Rep rows 5–8.
Rows 13 and 14 Rep rows 5 and 6.
Row 15 (WS) With C, *k3, MB, k2; rep from * to last st, k1. Push bobbles through to RS.
Row 16 With C, knit.
Rows 17–24 Rep rows 5–12.
Rep rows 1–24 for pat st.

BAG
BASE
(make 2)
With larger needles and A, cast on 25 sts. Knit 46 rows. Bind off, but do not fasten off last loop.

PANEL 1
Counting loop as 1 st, pick up and k 24 sts evenly along 1 side of base—25 sts.

BEGIN PAT ST
Work rows 1–24 of pat st twice, then rep rows 1–2 once more.
Next row (WS) With B, knit.
Next (eyelet) row K8, yo, k2tog, k5, yo, k to end.
Rep rows 5–14 once more, then rows 3–5 once. Bind off.

PANEL 2
Pick up and k 25 sts along opposite edge and work as for panel 1.

FINISHING
Place 2nd base on top of 1st base so that the 4 panels form 4 sides of bag. Sew the bases tog. Sew the sides of panels tog.

LINING
Cut 4 panels, each 6"/15cm wide and 7¾"/19.5cm long. Cut a base 6 x 6"/ 15 x 15cm.

On RS of fabric, mark for 2 buttonholes on each panel 1½"/4cm from top edge and 2¼"/5.5cm from each side. Place small piece of interfacing under each mark and make ½"/1.5cm buttonhole. Cut away the interfacing around the buttonhole and carefully cut buttonhole open.

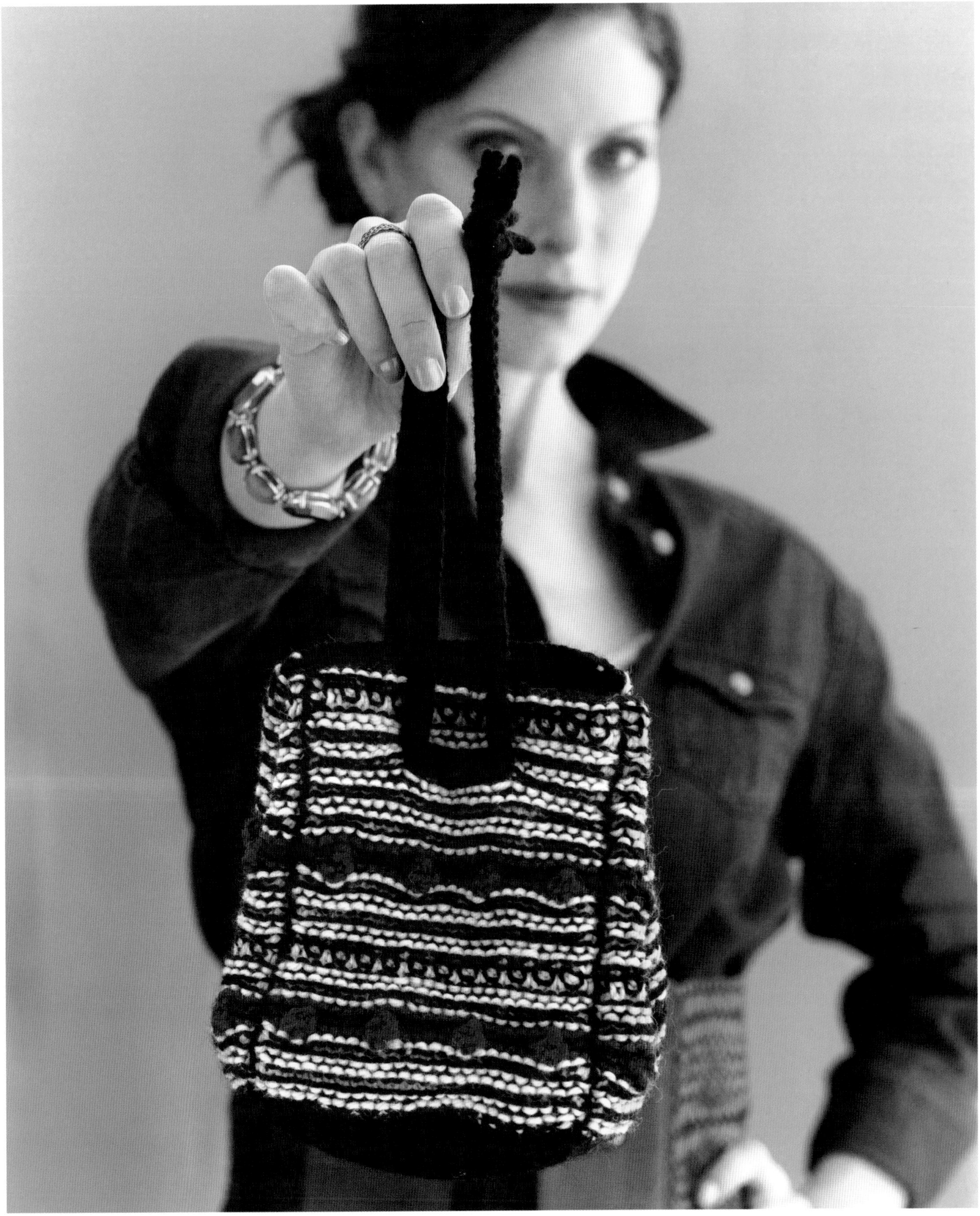

Place RS of 1st and 2nd panels tog and sew ½"/1.5cm seam. Rep for rem panel seams. Press seams open. Sew base lining to lower edge of panels. Insert lining into bag with WS tog. Match seams and pin edge of lining so it is below edge of bag. Sew lining to edge of bag.

CORDS
(make 2)
With smaller needles and A, cast on 142 sts. Knit 2 rows. Bind off. Weave 1 cord through eyelets and buttonhole on one panel of bag, then through opposite panel. Tie ends of cord tog. Rep on other side of bag for 2nd cord. ■

Pop of Color Project Bag

Bright bobbles stand out against black and white on a striking bag roomy enough to hold your latest project—see the matching accessories bag on page 66.

Designed by Jeannie Chin

KNITTED MEASUREMENTS
12¾ x 7½ x 7½"/32.5 x 19 x 19cm

MATERIALS
■ Three 3½oz/100g skeins (each approx 220yd/201m) of Universal Yarn *Deluxe Worsted* (100% wool) in #1900 ebony (A)

■ 2 skeins in #12270 natural (B)

■ 1 skein in #3691 Christmas red (C)

■ One pair each sizes 4 and 6 (3.5 and 4mm) needles OR SIZE TO OBTAIN GAUGE

■ ¾yd/.75m black cotton fabric

■ ⅛yd/.125m black lightweight interfacing for eyelets

■ Sewing needle and black thread

■ Note that no additional materials are needed for matching accessories bag on page 66

GAUGE
20 sts and 44 rows = 4"/10cm over garter st using larger needles.
TAKE TIME TO CHECK GAUGE.

STITCH GLOSSARY
MB (make bobble) (K1, yo, k1) in same st, turn, k3, turn, p3, turn, k3, turn, S2KP.
LS (long st) Insert RH needle through purl loop 2 rows below and knit it tog with next st on needle.

PATTERN STITCH
(multiple of 6 sts plus 1)
Rows 1 and 2 With A, knit.
Row 3 With B, knit.
Row 4 (RS) With B, *k1, LS; rep from * to last st, k1.
Rows 5 and 6 With A, knit.
Rows 7 and 8 With B, knit.
Rows 9–12 Rep rows 5–8.
Rows 13 and 14 Rep rows 5 and 6.
Row 15 (WS) With C, *k3, MB, k2; rep from * to last st, k1. Push bobbles through to RS.
Row 16 With C, knit.
Rows 17–24 Rep rows 5–12.
Rep rows 1–24 for pat st.

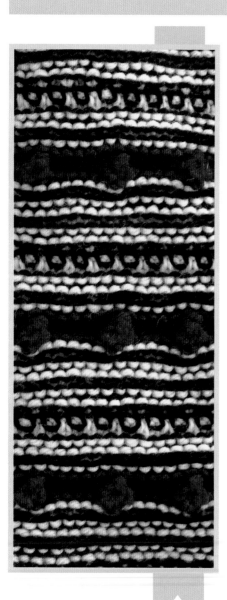

BAG

BASE
(make 2)

With larger needles and A, cast on 37 sts. Knit 71 rows. Bind off, but do not fasten off last loop.

PANEL 1

Counting loop as 1 st, pick up and k 36 sts evenly along 1 side of base—37 sts.

BEGIN PAT ST

Work rows 1–24 of pat st 4 times, then rep rows 1–14 once more.

Next row (WS) With B, knit.

Next (eyelet) row K12, yo, k2tog, k9, yo, k to end.

Rep rows 5–12 three times, then rep rows 1–3 once more. Bind off.

PANEL 2

Pick up and k 37 sts along opposite edge and work as for panel 1.

FINISHING

Place 2nd base on top of 1st base so that the 4 panels form 4 sides of bag. Sew the bases tog. Sew the sides of panels tog.

LINING

Cut 4 panels and a base, each 8½ x 8½"/21.5 x 21.5cm.

On RS of fabric, mark for 2 buttonholes on each panel, 2½"/6.5cm from top edge and 3"/7.5cm from each side. Place small piece of interfacing under each mark and make ½"/1.5cm buttonhole. Cut away the interfacing around the buttonhole and carefully cut buttonhole open.

Place RS of 1st and 2nd panels tog and sew ½"/1.5cm seam. Rep for rem panel seams. Press seams open. Sew base lining to lower edge of panels. Insert lining into bag with WS tog. Match seams and pin edge of lining so it is below edge of bag. Sew lining to edge of bag.

CORDS

(make 2)

With smaller needles and A, cast on 214 sts. Knit 2 rows. Bind off.

Weave 1 cord through eyelets and buttonhole on one panel of bag, then through opposite panel. Tie ends of cord tog. Rep on other side of bag for 2nd cord. ■

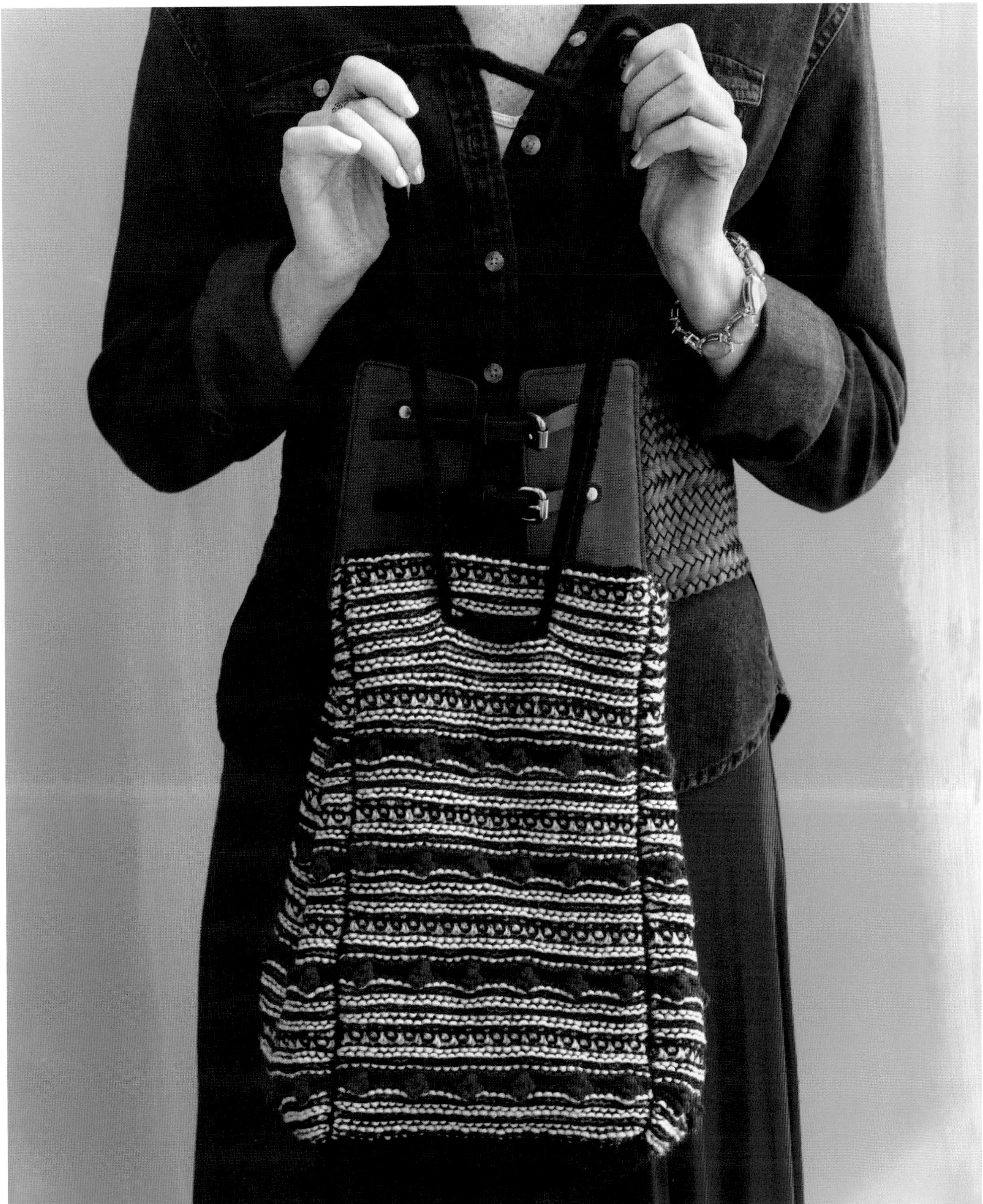

Swirled Cables Hat

Wide traveling cables on a garter stitch background, knit with the yarn held double, make this a quick knit and a snug and toasty topper.

Designed by Wilma Peers

SIZE
Adult woman

KNITTED MEASUREMENTS
Brim circumference 20"/51cm
Length 9½"/24cm

MATERIALS
■ One 3½oz/100g skein (each approx 220yd/201m) of Universal Yarn *Deluxe Worsted* (wool) in #3677 cobalt

■ One pair size 10.75 (7mm) needles OR SIZE TO OBTAIN GAUGE

■ Cable needle (cn)

■ Stitch markers

GAUGE
20 sts and 28 rows = 4"/10cm over pat st using size 10.75 (7mm) needles.
TAKE TIME TO CHECK GAUGE.

STITCH GLOSSARY
8-st RC Sl 4 sts to cn, hold to *back*, k4, k4 from cn.

NOTE
Yarn is held double throughout.

HAT
With 2 strands of yarn held tog, cast on 97 sts. Knit 3 rows.

BEGIN PATTERN ST
Row 1 (WS) Knit.
Row 2 (RS) K1, [M1, 8-st RC, k2tog, k9] 5 times, k1.
Rep rnds 1 and 2 for pat st until hat measures 5½"/14cm from beg, end with a row 2.

SHAPE CROWN
Row 1 and all WS rows through row 17 Knit.
Row 2 (RS) K1, [M1, 8-st RC, k2tog, k2tog, k7] 5 times, k1—92 sts.
Row 4 K1, [M1, 8-st RC, k2tog, k2tog, k6] 5 times, k1—87 sts.
Row 6 K1, [M1, 8-st RC, k2tog, k2tog, k5] 5 times, k1—82 sts.
Row 8 K1, [M1, 8-st RC, k2tog, k2tog, k4] 5 times, k1—77 sts.
Row 10 K1, [M1, 8-st RC, k2tog, k2tog, k3] 5 times, k1—72 sts.
Row 12 K1, [M1, 8-st RC, k2tog, k2tog, k2] 5 times, k1—67 sts.
Row 14 K1, [M1, 8-st RC, k2tog, k2tog, k1] 5 times, k1—62 sts.
Row 16 K1, [M1, 8-st RC, k2tog, k2tog] 5 times, k1—57 sts.
Row 18 K1, [M1, 8-st RC, k2tog, k1] 5 times, k1.
Row 19 (WS) K1, [ssk, k6, k2tog, k1] 5 times, k1—47 sts.
Row 20 K1, [8-st RC, k1] 5 times, k1.

Row 21 K1, [ssk, k7] 5 times, k1—42 sts.
Row 22 K5, [8-st RC] 4 times, k5.
Row 23 Knit.
Row 24 K1, *k2tog; rep from * to last st, k1—22 sts.
Row 25 Knit.
Row 26 K1, *k2tog, rep from * to last st, k1—12 sts.
Row 27 K1, [k2tog] 5 times, k1—7 sts.
Break yarn, leaving long tail. Draw through rem sts and secure.

FINISHING
Sew back seam. ■

Baby Kimono

Cute as well as cozy: a slip stitch pattern adds texture and colorplay to a simply shaped kimono wrap cardigan.

Designed by Sandi Rosner

SIZES
6 months (12 months, 18 months, 24 months)
Shown in size 6 months

KNITTED MEASUREMENTS
Chest (buttoned) 18¾ (19½, 21¼, 22)"/47.5 (49.5, 54, 56)cm
Length 8½ (9, 9½, 10)"/21.5 (23, 24, 25.5)cm

MATERIALS
■ 1 (1, 2, 2) 3½oz/100g skeins (each approx 220yd/201m) of Universal Yarn *Deluxe Worsted Superwash* (100% wool) in #701 rosy mauve (A)

■ 1 skein in #732 icy grey (B)

■ One each sizes 7 and 8 (4.5 and 5mm) circular needles, 24"/60cm long, OR SIZE TO OBTAIN GAUGE

■ One ⅝"/15mm button

■ One size 3 snap set

■ Stitch markers

GAUGE
20 sts and 36 rows = 4"/10cm over garter slip st using larger needle.
TAKE TIME TO CHECK GAUGE.

GARTER SLIP STITCH
(over an odd number of sts)
Row 1 (RS) With A, knit.
Row 2 With A, knit.
Row 3 With B, k1, *sl 1 wyib, k1; rep from * to end.
Row 4 Rep row 3.
Rep rows 1–4 for garter slip st.

BODY
With smaller needle and A, cast on 125 (133, 141, 149) sts.
Row 1 (RS) Purl.
Row 2 (WS) Knit.
Rep last 2 rows once more.
Hem joining row (RS) *Insert RH needle through next st, then through corresponding st at cast-on edge, and knit these sts tog; rep from * to end.
Change to larger needle.
Beg with row 2, work in garter slip st until piece measures 3½ (3¾, 4, 4¼)"/9 (9.5, 10, 11)cm from beg, end with a row 4 of pat.
Next row (buttonhole RS) Work 3 sts in pat, k2tog, yo, work in pat to end.
Next row Work in pat.
Next row Work 4 sts in pat, knit into the yo 2 rows below, work in pat to end.
Work 3 rows more in pat.

SHAPE FRONT NECK AND ARMHOLES
Note Read carefully before beg to knit; neck and armholes are shaped simultaneously.
Bind off 2 sts at beg of next 8 rows—109 (117, 125, 133) sts.

Next row (RS) Bind off 2 sts, work until 25 (28, 29, 32) sts are on RH needle, bind off 8 (8, 10, 10) sts for right armhole, work until 39 (41, 43, 45) sts are on RH needle for back, bind off 8 (8, 10, 10) sts for left armhole, work to end.

LEFT FRONT
Leaving back and right front sts on hold, cont on 27 (30, 31, 34) sts for left front only as foll:
Bind off 2 sts at neck edge (beg of WS rows) 5 (6, 4, 6) times—17 (18, 23, 22) sts.
Dec row (RS) Work in pat to last 3 sts, k2tog, k1—1 st dec'd.
Rep dec row every other row 8 (8, 12, 11) times more—8 (9, 10, 10) sts.
Work even until armhole measures 3½ (3¾, 4, 4¼)"/9 (9.5, 10, 11)cm, end with a WS row. Bind off.

RIGHT FRONT
Rejoin yarn to 25 (28, 29, 32) sts for right front at armhole edge ready to work a WS row. Work 1 WS row. Bind off 2 sts at neck edge (beg of RS rows) 4 (5, 3, 5) times—17 (18, 23, 22) sts. Work 1 WS row.
Dec row (RS) K1, ssk, work in pat to end—1 st dec'd.
Rep dec row every other row 8 (8, 12, 11) times more—8 (9, 10, 10) sts.
Work even until armhole measures 3½ (3¾, 4, 4¼)"/9 (9.5, 10, 11)cm, end with a WS row. Bind off.

BACK

Rejoin yarn to 39 (41, 43, 45) sts for back ready to work a WS row. Work even in pat until armhole measures 3½ (3¾, 4, 4¼)"/9 (9.5, 10, 11)cm, end with a WS row. Bind off.

SLEEVES

With smaller needle and A, cast on 25 (25, 29, 29) sts.

Work as for body through hem joining row. Change to larger needle.

Beg with row 2, work 3 rows in garter slip st.

Inc row (RS) K1, kfb, work in pat to last st, kfb, k1—2 sts inc'd.

Working incs into pat, rep inc row every 8th row 4 (6, 5, 6) times more—35 (39, 41, 43) sts.

Work even until sleeve measures 6½ (7½, 8½, 12)"/16.5 (19, 21.5, 30.5)cm from beg, end with a WS row and mark each end of last row for cap.

Work even until piece measures 1 (1, 1¼, 1¼)"/2.5 (2.5, 3, 3)cm from markers. Bind off.

FINISHING

Block lightly to finished measurements. Sew shoulder seams. Sew sleeves into armholes, sewing caps above markers along bound-off edges of body. Sew sleeve seams.

NECK EDGING

With RS facing, smaller needle and A, beg at lower edge, pick up and k 1 st for every 2 rows along right front edge to neck shaping, then pick up and k 1 st for every bound-off st and 2 sts for every 3 rows along right front neck to shoulder seam. Pick up and k 1 st for every bound-off st along back neck edge, then pick up and k as for right front edge along left front edge to lower edge.

Row 1 (WS) Knit.

Row 2 Purl.

Rep rows 1 and 2 once, then rep row 1 once more. Bind off. Fold edge to WS and sew bound-off edge neatly in place.

Sew one half of snap set to left front near beg of neck shaping. Sew rem half in corresponding position on WS of right front. Sew button to left front to correspond to buttonhole. ■

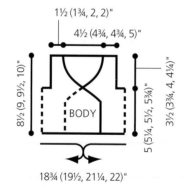

1½ (1¾, 2, 2)"

4½ (4¾, 4¾, 5)"

8½ (9, 9½, 10)"

BODY

3½ (3¾, 4, 4¼)"

5 (5¼, 5½, 5¾)"

18¾ (19½, 21¼, 22)"

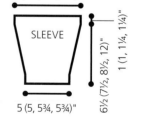

7 (7¾, 8¼, 8½)"

SLEEVE

1 (1, 1¼, 1¼)"

6½ (7½, 8½, 12)"

5 (5, 5¾, 5¾)"

Puppy & Kitten Hand Puppets

Easy-to-knit furry friends come to life as puppets perfect for little hands and big imaginations.

Designed by Phyllis Rowley

SIZE
Small child

KNITTED MEASUREMENTS
Circumference 7 (9)"/18 (23)cm
Length 8 (10)"/20.5 (25.5)cm

MATERIALS
■ One 3½oz/100g skein (each approx 220yd/201m) of Universal Yarn *Deluxe Worsted Superwash* (100% wool) each in #733 sweatshirt grey (A), #728 pulp (B), #735 ebony (C), and #725 adobe (D)

■ Small amounts in #743 bashful pink (E), #744 blue lagoon (F), and #727 chocolate (G)

■ One pair size 8 (5mm) needles OR SIZE TO OBTAIN GAUGE

GAUGE
18 sts and 38 rows = 4"/10cm over garter st using size 8 (5mm) needles. TAKE TIME TO CHECK GAUGE.

NOTE
The yarn amounts listed will make both puppets shown, with plenty to spare.

PUPPET BODY

(make 2 for each puppet)

FOR KITTEN (PUPPY)

With A (D), cast on 15 sts.
Knit 4 rows.
*K 2 rows B, k 2 rows A (D); rep from * for stripe pat until piece measures 6"/15cm from beg, end with a WS row.

SHAPE MOUTH

Next (dec) row (RS) K1, k2tog, k to end of row—1 st dec'd.
Rep dec row *every* row 9 times more—5 sts. Bind off.

MOUTH

With E, cast on 5 sts.
Next (inc) row (RS) K1, kfb, k to end of row—1 st inc'd.
Rep inc row *every* row 9 times more—15 sts. Knit 2 rows.

Next (dec) row (RS) K1, k2tog, k to end of row—1 st dec'd.
Rep dec row *every* row 9 times more—5 sts. Bind off.

FINISHING

Sew the 2 body pieces tog from lower edge to beg of mouth shaping to form a tube. Sew in the mouth.

EYES

With C (G), cast on 4 sts. Knit 8 rows. Bind off. Sew cast-on edge to bound-off edge. Sew to head of puppet, using photo as guide.

EARS FOR CAT

With C (A), cast on 1 st.
Row 1 (RS) Kfb—2 sts.
Row 2 Knit.
Row 3 [Kfb] twice—4 sts.
Row 4 Knit.

Row 5 (inc) K1, kfb, k to last 2 sts, kfb, k1—2 sts inc'd.
Rep last 2 rows 3 times more—12 sts. Bind off.
Align bound-off edge of ear perpendicular to side seam of puppet even with mouth opening and sew down, creating a small fold in the center of the ear.

WHISKERS AND NOSE

With C, cast on 1 st, *k1, do not turn, sl st back to LH needle; rep from * until whisker is desired length. Fasten off. Rep for 3 more whiskers. Sew to puppet face, using photo as guide.
With C, embroider several straight sts at point of face, using photo as guide.

EARS FOR PUPPY

With D, cast on 10 sts. Work even in garter st for 2"/5cm.
Next (dec) row (RS) K1, k2tog, k to last 3 sts, k2tog, k1—2 sts dec'd.
Rep dec row *every* row twice more. Bind off. Sew cast-on edge of ear to puppet head, using photo as guide.

TONGUE FOR PUPPY

With E, cast on 5 sts. Work in garter st for 1½"/4cm. Bind off. Sew to center of mouth.

NECK TIE FOR PUPPY

With F, cast on 3 sts. Work in garter st for 12"/30.5cm. Bind off.
Tack center of piece to back neck and tie in knot in front.

SCARF FOR KITTEN

With F, cast on 3 sts. Work in garter st for 12"/30.5cm.
Next row K1, drop next st, k1, pass first st over last st and fasten off. Let dropped st unravel.
Tack center of piece to back neck, wrap twice around neck, and tie in knot in front. ■

Chevron & Striped Pillow

This pillow has a side to suit each side of you: stripes for when you're in a straight-arrow mood and a chevron pattern for when you're feeling ziggy.

Designed by Dorcas Sokolow

KNITTED MEASUREMENTS
20 x 20"/50 x 50cm

MATERIALS
Colorway 1
■ One 3½oz/100g skein (each approx 220yd/201m) of Universal Yarn *Deluxe Worsted* (100% wool) each in #14007 indigo (A), #12236 violet glow (B), 12182 gold spice (C), #12404 beeswax (D), and #12270 natural (E)

Colorway 2
■ One 3½oz/100g skein (each approx 220yd/201m) of Universal Yarn *Deluxe Worsted* (100% wool) each in #14007 indigo (A), #12176 teal viper (B), 12256 tangerine flash (C), #12270 natural (D), and #12404 beeswax (E)

■ One pair size 8 (5mm) needles OR SIZE TO OBTAIN GAUGE

■ 20"/50cm pillow form

GAUGE
20 sts and 36 rows = 4"/10cm over garter st using size 8 (5mm) needles. TAKE TIME TO CHECK GAUGE.

STRIPE PATTERN
*8 rows A, 8 rows B, 8 rows C, 8 rows D, 8 rows E; rep from * for color pat.

CHEVRON SIDE
With A, cast on 99 sts.
Begin color pat.
Row 1 (RS) Knit.
Row 2 K2tog, k2, *M1, k1, M1, k3, k3tog, k3; rep from * 8 times more, M1, k1, M1, k2, k2tog.
Rep rows 1 and 2 for chevron pat, AT THE SAME TIME, cont in stripe pat until piece measures 20"/50cm from beg. Bind off.

STRIPE SIDE
With A, cast on 99 sts. Work in garter st and stripe pat until piece measures same as chevron side. Bind off.

FINISHING
Sew 3 sides of pillow tog. Insert pillow form and sew 4th side. ■

Scallop Stripe Scarf

A simple garter stitch scarf transforms into an interplay of movement and color, with scallop stripes formed by increases and decreases.

Designed by Carol J. Sulcoski

KNITTED MEASUREMENTS
Approx 7¼ x 72"/18.5 x 182.5cm

MATERIALS
■ Two 3½oz/100g skeins (each approx 220yd/201m) of Universal Yarn *Deluxe Worsted* (100% wool) in #12508 woodsy heather (A)

■ One skein each in #13105 straw (B) and #12507 shamrock (C)

■ One pair size 9 (5.5mm) needles OR SIZE TO OBTAIN GAUGE

■ Spare size 9 (5.5mm) needle

■ Crochet hook for fringe

GAUGE
18 sts and 32 rows = 4"/10cm over garter st using size 9 (5.5mm) needles. TAKE TIME TO CHECK GAUGE.

3-NEEDLE BIND-OFF
1) Hold right sides of pieces together on 2 needles. Insert 3rd needle knitwise into first st of each needle, and wrap yarn knitwise.
2) Knit these 2 sts together, and slip them off the needles. *Knit the next 2 sts together in the same manner.
3) Slip first st on 3rd needle over 2nd st and off needle. Rep from * in step 2 across row until all sts are bound off.

NOTE
Scarf is worked in two halves, then grafted at center using Kitchener st or 3-needle bind-off. It is also acceptable to bind off both halves and seam them together.

FIRST HALF OF SCARF
With A, cast on 33 sts. Knit 11 rows.
Row 12 (WS) With B, purl.
Row 13 (RS) With B, *k2tog, k2, kfb, kfb, k3, ssk; rep from * to end.
Row 14 With A, purl.
With A, knit 7 rows.
Rows 22–24 Rep rows 12–14.
With A, knit 3 rows.
Row 28 With C, purl.
Row 29 With C, rep row 13.
Row 30 With A, purl.
With A, knit 7 rows.
Rows 38–40 Rep rows 12–14.
With A, knit 7 rows.
Rows 48–50 Rep rows 12–14.
With A only, work in garter st (k every row) until piece measures 36"/91.5cm from beg, end with a WS row. Place sts on spare needle.

SECOND HALF OF SCARF
Work as for first half, reversing placement of B and C stripes.

FINISHING
Graft scarf halves at center using 3-needle bind-off. Block lightly to measurements.

FRINGE
Cut 90 lengths each of B and C approx 18"/45.5cm long. Hold 3 strands together for each fringe, alternating 2 strands of B with 1 strand of C and vice versa. Fold 3 strands in half to form a loop. With crochet hook, pull the loop through 1 st on cast-on edge of scarf. Pull ends of strands through loop and pull to tighten. Attach 15 fringes to each end of scarf. ■

Mobius Hat

A mobius twist worked in the cast-on rounds creates a jaunty turned-up brim on this fresh and flattering topper.

Designed by Candace Eisner Strick

KNITTED MEASUREMENTS
Head circumference 21"/53.5cm
Length 8½"/21.5cm

MATERIALS
■ One 3½oz/100g skein (each approx 220yd/201m) of Universal Yarn *Deluxe Worsted* (100% wool) each in #12224 chartreuse olive (A) and #12181 brown bronze (B)

■ One each sizes 3 and 7 (3.25 and 4.5mm) circular needles, 47"/120cm long, OR SIZE TO OBTAIN GAUGE

■ One size 7 (4.5mm) circular needle, 16"/40cm long

■ One set (5) size 7 (4.5mm) double-pointed needles (dpns)

■ Stitch markers

GAUGE
19 sts and 40 rnds = 4"/10cm over garter st using larger needle.
TAKE TIME TO CHECK GAUGE.

STITCH GLOSSARY
CD (central decrease) Sl 2 sts tog knitwise, sl 1 st purlwise, insert LH needle through fronts of all 3 sts and k3tog—2 sts dec'd.

NOTE
Carry unused color loosely up WS of work.

HAT
Cast on using mobius cast-on as foll:
With smaller 47"/120cm needle and A, place a slip knot on needle. Using backward loop method, cast on 100 sts—101 sts including slip knot. Turn the sts so they are facing upward (with what was the lower edge of each cast-on st at the top) and slide them to flexible part of circular needle. Insert RH needle into each top loop from back to front, allowing flexible part of needle to double around itself, crossing over at just one point. Turn work so working yarn is coming from RH needle—201 sts. Place marker (pm) for beg of rnd.
Rnd 1 With A, p101, [remount next st so that the right leg is in front of needle (untwisted) and purl it] 100 times.
Change to larger 47"/120cm needle.
Cont in garter st (k 1 rnd, p 1 rnd), work in stripe sequence as foll: 2 rnds A, then 3 rnds B, 3 rnds A, 3 rnds B, 1 rnd A.
Next rnd With 16"/40cm needle and A, k50, bind off next 101 sts, bring the lower needle to the top needle, k50—100 sts. With A, purl 1 rnd, then cont in garter st, work [3 rnds B, 3 rnds A] twice, then 5 rnds A, 3 rnds B, 3 rnds A, ending last rnd 1 st before marker. Place new marker for beg of rnd.

SHAPE CROWN
Note Change to dpns when there are too few sts to fit comfortably on circular needle.
Rnd 1 With B, [CD, p22] 4 times—92 sts.
Rnd 2 With B, k to 1 st before marker.
Note Move beg-of-rnd marker to right of first CD on rnd 3 and all subsequent dec rnds.
Rnd 3 With B, [CD, p20] 4 times—84 sts.
Rnd 4 With A, rep rnd 2.
Rnd 5 With A, [CD, p18] 4 times—76 sts.
Rnd 6 With A, rep rnd 2.
Rnd 7 With B, [CD, p16] 4 times—68 sts.
Rnd 8 With B, rep rnd 2.
Rnd 9 With B, [CD, p14] 4 times—60 sts.
Rnd 10 With A, rep rnd 2.
Rnd 11 With A, [CD, p12] 4 times—52 sts.
Rnd 12 With A, rep rnd 2.
Rnd 13 With B, [CD, p10] 4 times—44 sts.
Rnd 14 With B, rep rnd 2.
Rnd 15 With B, [CD, p8] 4 times—36 sts. Cut B and work to end in A only.
Rnd 16 With A, rep rnd 2.
Rnd 17 [CD, p6] 4 times—28 sts.
Rnd 18 Rep rnd 2.
Rnd 19 [CD, p4] 4 times—20 sts.
Rnd 20 Rep rnd 2.
Rnd 21 [CD, p2] 4 times—12 sts.
Rnd 22 Rep rnd 2.
Rnd 23 [CD] 4 times—4 sts.
Break yarn, leaving long tail. Draw tail through rem 4 sts and secure on WS. ■

Eyelet Slippers

Feminine details make these slippers a pretty pair: a fan stitch at the toe and heel, eyelet trim, and a crochet chain tied in a bow.

Designed by Nina Brown

SIZE
Adult woman

KNITTED MEASUREMENTS
Length from heel to toe 9½"/23cm
Length from cuff to heel 4"/10cm

MATERIALS
■ One 3½oz/100g skein (each approx 220yd/201m) of Universal Yarn *Deluxe Worsted* (100% wool) in #14018 rhapsody

■ One pair size 7 (4.5mm) needles OR SIZE TO OBTAIN GAUGE

■ Size G/6 (4mm) crochet hook

■ Stitch markers

GAUGE
18 sts and 36 rows = 4"/10cm over garter st using size 7 (4.5mm) needles. TAKE TIME TO CHECK GAUGE.

SHORT ROW WRAP AND TURN (W&T)
on RS row (on WS row)
1) Wyib (wyif), sl next st purlwise.
2) Move yarn between the needles to the front (back).
3) Sl the same st back to LH needle. Turn work. One st is wrapped.

STITCH GLOSSARY
Kfbf Knit into the (front, back, front) of next st—2 sts inc'd.

SLIPPERS
SOLE
Cast on 59 sts.
Row 1 (WS) K25, place marker (pm), k9, pm, k to end.
Row 2 (inc) K to marker, sl marker, k4, kfbf, k4, sl marker, k to end—2 sts inc'd.
Row 3 Knit.
Rep last 2 rows 5 times more, working kfbf into center st between markers every other row—71 sts total, 21 sts between markers. Knit 2 rows even.

UPPER
Row 1 (dec) K2tog, k to last 2 sts, k2tog—69 sts.
Row 2 Knit.
Row 3 (dec WS) K2tog, k to marker, sl marker, k2, yo, k2tog, k13, k2tog, yo, k2, sl marker, k to last 2 sts, k2tog—67 sts.
Row 4 (RS) K to marker, sl marker, k2, kfb in yo, k15, kfb in yo, k2, sl marker, k to end—69 sts, 23 sts between markers.
Row 5 Rep row 1—67 sts, 23 between markers.
Row 6 Knit.

BEGIN SHORT ROW TOE SHAPING
Row 7 (short row) K2tog, k to marker, sl marker, k2, [yo, k2tog] twice, k11, [k2tog, yo] twice, k2, sl marker, w&t, sl marker.

Row 8 (short row) K2, kfb in yo, k1, kfb in yo, k13, kfb in yo, k1, kfb in yo, k2, sl marker, w&t, sl marker—27 sts between markers.
Row 9 (short row) K to marker, sl marker, k1, w&t.
Row 10 (short row) K1, sl marker, k7, [yo twice, k1] 14 times, k6, sl marker, k1, w&t.
Row 11 (short row) K1, sl marker, k2, [yo, k2tog] twice, yo, sl next 15 sts, dropping extra wraps, sl 15 sts back to LH needle and k15tog, [yo, k2tog] twice, yo, k2, sl marker, k2, w&t.
Row 12 K2, sl marker, k1, [k1, kfb in yo] 3 times, k1, [kfb in yo, k1] 3 times, k1, sl marker, k to last 2 sts, k2tog—63 sts, 21 sts between markers.
Row 13 K to marker, sl marker, [k2tog] 5 times, yo, k1, yo, [k2tog] 5 times, k to end—55 sts.
Row 14 Rep row 1, removing markers—53 sts.
Rows 15 and 16 Knit.
Row 17 K18, [k2tog] 4 times, k1, [k2tog] 4 times, k to end—45 sts.
Row 18 Rep row 1—43 sts.
Row 19 (eyelet row) [K2tog, yo] 10 times, S2KP, [yo, k2tog] 10 times—41 sts. Knit 1 row. Bind off.

HEEL
Cast on 27 sts. Knit 4 rows.
Row 5 K5, yo, k2tog, k13, k2tog, yo, k5.
Row 6 (inc RS) K5, kfb in yo, k15, kfb in yo, k5—29 sts.
Rows 7 and 8 Knit.

Row 9 K5, [yo, k2tog] twice, k11, [k2tog, yo] twice, k5.

Row 10 K4, [k1, kfb in yo] twice, k13, [kfb in yo, k1] twice, k4—33 sts.

Row 11 Knit.

Row 12 K10, [yo twice, k1] 14 times, k9.

Row 13 K4, [yo, k2tog] twice, yo, sl next 15 sts, dropping extra wraps, sl 15 sts back to LH needle and k15tog, [yo, k2tog] twice, yo, k5—21 sts.

Row 14 K4, [k1, kfb in yo] 3 times, k1, [kfb in yo, k1] 3 times, k4—27 sts. Knit 1 row.

Row 16 K13, yo, k1, yo, k13—29 sts.

Rows 17–20 Knit.

Row 21 K14, yo, k1, yo, k14—31 sts.

Rows 22–24 Knit.

Row 25 (eyelet row) [K2tog, yo] 7 times, S2KP, [yo, k2tog] 7 times—29 sts. Knit 1 row. Bind off.

FINISHING

Sew sole seam. Fold heel section in half and mark center. Align center of heel with sole seam and sew heel to sole and upper.

TIES

(make 2)
With hook, ch 100 sts. Fasten off. Knot each end.
Weave chain through eyelets at ankle and tie at front. ∎

Baby Garlands

Brighten up the nursery with these sweet and swingy garlands. Each flag is shaped by an eyelet heart pattern and adorned with a pompom and tassel.

Designed by Julie H. Rose

KNITTED MEASUREMENTS
Approx 23 or 40"/58.5 or 101.5cm

MATERIALS
Long garland
■ One 3½oz/100g skein (each approx 220yd/201m) of Universal Yarn *Deluxe Worsted Superwash* (100% wool) each in #721 honeysuckle (A) and #704 nectarine (B)

Short garland
■ One 3½oz/100g skein (each approx 220yd/201m) of Universal Yarn *Deluxe Worsted Superwash* (100% wool) each in #739 turquoise (A) and #712 shamrock smoothie (B)

■ Size 9 (5.5mm) circular needle, at least 16"/40cm long, OR SIZE TO OBTAIN GAUGE

■ One set (5) size 9 (5.5mm) double-pointed needles (dpns)

■ 1⅜"/3.5cm pompom maker (optional)

■ 3"/7.5cm square of cardboard for making tassels

GAUGE
One triangle measures approx 4¼ x 3"/11 x 7.5cm using size 9 (5.5mm) needles.
TAKE TIME TO CHECK GAUGE.

I-CORD

With 2 dpns, cast on 3 sts. *Knit one row. Without turning work, slide the sts back to the opposite end of needle to work next row from RS. Pull yarn tightly from the end of the row. Rep from * until cord is desired length.

TASSEL

Wrap yarn 26 times around cardboard. Break yarn, leaving an 8"/12.5cm tail. Slip yarn from cardboard, wrap tail several times tightly around tassel approx ¼"/.5cm from top, and tie off. With scissors, cut opposite end of tassel and trim ends.

NOTE

All triangles are worked and left on hold on circular needle, then joined with I-cord.

TRIANGLES

(make 4 in A, 3 in B for long garland, 2 in A, 1 in B for short garland)
With circular needle, cast on 2 sts, leaving 12"/30.5cm tail.
Row 1 K2.
Row 2 (RS) K1, M1, k1—3 sts.
Row 3 and all WS rows Knit.
Row 4 K1, M1, k2—4 sts.
Row 6 K2, yo, k2—5 sts.
Row 8 K2, yo, k1, yo, k2—7 sts.
Row 10 K2, yo, k3, yo, k2—9 sts.
Row 12 K2, yo, k5, yo, k2—11 sts.
Row 14 K2, yo, k7, yo, k2—13 sts.
Row 16 K2, yo, k4, yo, ssk, k3, yo, k2—15 sts.
Row 18 K2, yo, ssk, k3, yo, k1, yo, k3, k2tog, yo, k2—17 sts.

Row 20 K2, yo, ssk, k1, k2tog, yo, k3, yo, ssk, k1, k2tog, yo, k2.
Row 22 K3, yo, SK2P, yo, k5, yo, ssk, return dec'd st to LH needle, pass next st over dec'd st, sl st to RH needle, yo, k3.
Rows 23–25 Knit.
Break yarn, leaving 48"/122cm tail, and leave sts on hold on circular needle.

FINISHING
I-CORD EDGE

With dpn and A, cast on 3 sts and work a 5"/12.5cm I-cord. Break yarn.
Join B and join I-cord to first triangle worked as foll (long tail should be at left edge of triangle): *k2 from I-cord, ssk last st from I-cord tog with first st from triangle, slide these 3 sts back to RH needle, pulling yarn tightly from behind; rep from * until all sts along triangle are joined. Break B. Using A tail from first triangle, join next triangle in the same manner. Cont to work in this manner, using contrasting tail from previous triangle to join next triangle, until all triangles have been joined with I-cord. Join A and work 5"/12.5cm I-cord. Bind off as foll: k2tog, k1. Break yarn and pull through rem 2 sts.

Block lightly. Make 1⅜"/3.5cm pompoms in contrasting colors for each triangle, and tassels in matching colors for each triangle. Using photo as guide, attach pompoms to lower point using tail from cast-on, then wrap tail around corresponding tassel to secure. ■

Drop Stitch Cowl

Bands of two drop stitch patterns create movement and texture, and two colors help define those bands in a cowl that's knitted flat and seamed.

Designed by Wilma Peers

KNITTED MEASUREMENTS
Circumference 30"/76cm
Length 13"/33cm

MATERIALS
■ One 3½oz/100g skein (each approx 220yd/201m) of Universal Yarn *Deluxe Worsted* (100% wool) in #71662 turquoise (A)

■ One 1¾oz/50g skein (each approx 440yd/400m) of Universal Yarn/Fibra Natura *Whisper Lace* (70% wool, 30% silk) in #103 harbor (B)

■ One pair size 10.75 (7mm) needles OR SIZE TO OBTAIN GAUGE

■ Locking stitch marker or safety pin

GAUGE
15 sts and 18 rows = 4"/10cm over crossed drop st using size 10.75 (7mm) needles.
TAKE TIME TO CHECK GAUGE.

CROSSED DROP STITCH
(multiple of 8 sts)
Rows 1–6 Knit.
Row 7 (RS) *Yo twice, k1; rep from * to end.
Row 8 (WS) *Sl 4 sts to small stitch holder or safety pin and hold to front, dropping yarn overs, k4, dropping yarn

overs, pull small stitch holder or pin through long loops of sts just worked on RH needle, place 4 sts from holder or pin on LH needle, then k these 4 sts; rep from * to end.
Rep rows 1–8 for crossed drop st.

SIMPLE DROP STITCH
(over any number of sts)
Row 1 Knit.
Row 2 *Yo, k1; rep from * to end.
Row 3 *K1, dropping wrap; rep from * to end.
Row 4 Knit.
Rep rows 1–4 for simple drop st.

COWL
With A, cast on 112 sts. *With A, work rows 1–8 of crossed drop st twice, with 2 strands of B held tog, work rows 1–4 of simple drop st twice; rep from * once more. With A, work rows 1–8 of crossed drop st twice. Bind off loosely.

FINISHING
Seam edges to form cowl, seaming only garter st sections to allow openwork to remain. ■

Zigzag Mitts

A zigzag cable pattern on a garter stitch background adds
a funky vibe to a snug-fitting pair of mitts.

◆

Designed by Cheryl Murray

SIZES
Small/Medium and Large
Shown in size Small/Medium

KNITTED MEASUREMENTS
Palm circumference 6½ (7½)"/
15 (19)cm
Length 8"/20.5cm

MATERIALS
▧ One 3½oz/100g skein (each
approx 220yd/201m) of Universal
Yarn *Deluxe Worsted* (100% wool)
in #3608 marigold

▧ One set (5) size 6 (4mm)
double-pointed needles (dpns)
OR SIZE TO OBTAIN GAUGE

▧ Stitch markers

▧ Scrap yarn

GAUGE
22 sts and 40 rnds = 4"/10cm over
chart pat using size 6 (4mm) needles.
TAKE TIME TO CHECK GAUGE.

STITCH GLOSSARY
2-st RC Sl next st to cn and hold to *back*,
k1, k1 from cn.
2-st LC Sl next st to cn and hold to *front*,
k1, k1 from cn.

LEFT MITT
CUFF
Cast on 36 (42) sts. Join, being careful
not to twist sts, and place marker (pm)
for beg of rnd.

BEGIN CHART
Rnd 1 Work 6-st rep 6 (7) times around.
Cont to foll chart in this manner until
rnd 16 is complete.

SHAPE GUSSET
Note Gusset sts between markers are
worked in garter st (k 1 rnd, p 1 rnd).
Next rnd M1, pm, work to end of rnd—
37 (43) sts.
Work 1 rnd even.
Next (inc) rnd Kfb, sl marker, work
to end of rnd—38 sts.
Work 1 rnd even.
Next (inc) rnd Kfb, k to marker, sl
marker, work to end of rnd—1 st inc'd.
Rep inc rnd every other rnd 9 (11) times
more—12 (14) sts between markers,
48 (50) sts in rnd.
Work even until rnd 16 is complete.

HAND
Place 12 (14) gusset sts on scrap yarn
for thumb.
Work rnds 1–16 once more. Piece
measures approx 8"/20.5cm from beg.
Bind off loosely in pat.

THUMB
Pick up and k 1 st along thumb opening,
place 12 (14) thumb sts on dpns, pick up
and k 1 st along thumb opening, pm for
beg of rnd—14 (16) sts.
Next (dec) rnd K2tog, k to last 2 sts,
k2tog—12 (14) sts.
Beg with a purl rnd, work 8 rnds in garter
st. Bind off loosely purlwise.

RIGHT MITT
Work as for left mitt to Shape Gusset.
Next rnd Work to end of rnd, pm,
M1—37 (43) sts.
Work 1 rnd even.
Next (inc) rnd Work to marker,
sl marker, kfb—38 (44) sts.
Work 1 rnd even.
Next (inc) rnd Work to marker,
sl marker, kfb, work to end of rnd—
1 st inc'd.
Complete as for left mitt. ■

STITCH KEY

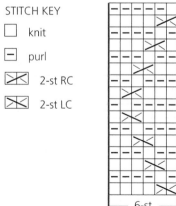

knit

— purl

⊠ 2-st RC

⊠ 2-st LC

6-st
rep

Rag Doll

Every girl needs a doll to cuddle with, and charming details will make this a special favorite: a colorful outfit, a sweet face, and fluffy hair tied with a bow.

Designed by Lori Steinberg

KNITTED MEASUREMENTS
Length from head to toe, not including hair 14"/35.5cm
Body circumference, stuffed, approx 8"/20.5cm

MATERIALS
■ One 3½oz/100g skein (each approx 220yd/201m) of Universal Yarn *Deluxe Worsted* (100% wool) each in #12298 butter (A), #71051 toast (B), and #1900 ebony (C)

■ Small amounts each in #14005 orchid (D) and #71662 turquoise (E)

■ One pair each sizes 6 and 8 (4 and 5mm) needles OR SIZE TO OBTAIN GAUGE

■ Stuffing

■ Tapestry needle

GAUGE
23 sts and 40 rows = 4"/10cm over garter st using smaller needles.
TAKE TIME TO CHECK GAUGE.

NOTE
All pieces are worked flat and seamed. The arms, legs, and skirt are each made in one piece and folded in half before seaming. The body and head are made up of 2 pieces each.

DOLL BODY
(make 2)
Note Color change at top of body is worked using separate bobbins for each color section. Do not carry colors across WS of work. Wind off a small amount of A before beginning.
With smaller needles and A, cast on 12 sts. Knit 2 rows.
Next row (RS) [Kfb] 12 times—24 sts. Work even until piece measures 4"/10cm from beg.

SHAPE SHOULDERS
Next (dec) row (RS) With A, SKP, k6, with B k8, join bobbin of A, k6, k2tog—22 sts.
Working colors as they appear, dec 1 st each side every other row 4 times more—14 sts. Bind off.

HEAD
(make 2, one with A and one with C)
With smaller needles and A (C), cast on 6 sts. Knit 1 row.
Next (inc) row (RS) [Kfb] 6 times—12 sts.
Knit 1 row.
Next (inc) row (RS) [Kfb] twice, k to last 2 sts, [kfb] twice—16 sts.
Knit 1 row.
Next (inc) row (RS) Kfb, k to last st, kfb—18 sts.
Rep last 2 rows once more—20 sts.
Knit 9 rows.

Next (dec) row (RS) SKP, k to last 2 sts, k2tog—18 sts.
Knit 1 row.
Rep last 2 rows once more—16 sts.
Next (dec) row (RS) [SKP] twice, k to last 4 sts, [k2tog] twice—12 sts.
Knit 1 row.
Next (dec) row (RS) [K2tog] 6 times—6 sts.
Knit 1 row. Bind off.

SHAPE SHOULDER

Dec 1 st each side every other row 3 times—8 sts.
Work 5 rows even.
Next (dec) row (RS) [K2tog] 4 times—4 sts.
Knit 1 row. Bind off.

LEGS

(make 2)
With smaller needles and D, cast on 10 sts.
Knit 1 row.
Next (inc) row (RS) [Kfb], k3, [kfb] twice, k3, kfb—14 sts.
Work even in garter st for 7 rows.
Next (dec) row (RS) [SKP, k3, k2tog] twice—10 sts.
Next (joint) row (WS) Purl.

BEGIN STRIPES

Cont in garter st, work [2 rows E, 2 rows A, 2 rows D] 3 times. Break all yarns.

KNEE AND UPPER LEG

With A, k 1 row, p 1 row, work 23 rows in garter st. Purl 1 WS row. Bind off.

SKIRT

Note Carry A up the side of work, break D and E after each stripe.
With larger needles and A, cast on 30 sts.
Knit 4 rows A, 2 rows E, 4 rows A, 2 rows D, 2 rows A.
Next (inc) row (RS) With A, k2, *kfb; rep from * to last 2 sts, k2—56 sts.
Knit 1 row A, 2 rows E, 10 rows A, 2 rows E. Break A and E.
With D, knit 2 rows.
Next (inc) row (RS) With D, k2, *kfb; rep from * to last 2 sts, k2—108 sts.
Knit 5 rows. Bind off.

ARMS

(make 2)
With smaller needles and B, cast on 10 sts.
Knit 1 row.
Next (inc) row (RS) [Kfb], k3, [kfb] twice, k3, kfb—14 sts.
Work even in garter st for 5 rows.
Next (dec) row (RS) [SKP, k3, k2tog] twice—10 sts.
Next (joint) row (WS) Purl.
Next (inc) row (RS) [Kfb], k3, [kfb] twice, k3, kfb—14 sts.
Work 12 rows even in garter st.
Next (joint) row (WS) Purl.
Work 10 rows in garter st.

FINISHING

With D, using photo as guide, embroider chain stitch around neck of dress.
With A, seam bottom and sides of body pieces tog. Stuff lightly. Sew closed.
Fold one arm in half and sew seam from shoulder to first joint. Stitch through both layers of fabric at joint. Sew seam to 2nd joint and stuff lower arm lightly. Stitch through both layers of fabric at joint. Lightly stuff hand and sew closed. Rep for other arm.
Stuff and seam legs in same manner.
Sew arms and legs to body.
Sew the 2 head pieces tog, leaving a small opening for stuffing. Stuff head and shape as desired. Sew closed. Sew head firmly to body.
Sew back seam of skirt. Slip skirt onto body and place where desired. Tack in place.

HAIR

Cut approx 64 strands of C 16"/40.5cm long. Holding 2 strands tog, fold in half and thread loop through tapestry needle. Insert tapestry needle through 1 stitch on B side of head seam and draw the fold of the strands through the stitch. Remove needle and pull ends of strands through the loop. Pull tight. Rep all around the seam of the head. Pull hair together in a high pony tail and tie with a length of D. Trim hair to taste.

MOUTH

With double strand of E, embroider mouth using 2 straight sts, using photo as guide for placement.

EYES

With double strand of D, work 1 French knot for each eye, using photo as guide for placement. ■

Wavy Drop Stitch Scarf

A quirky version of a drop stitch pattern scallops the side edges on a delicate scarf that will take you from fall through spring.

Designed by Amanda Blair Brown

KNITTED MEASUREMENTS
Approx 7 x 80"/18 x 203cm

MATERIALS
■ Two 3½oz/100g skeins (each approx 220yd/201m) of Universal Yarn *Deluxe Worsted* (100% wool) in #14008 cumulonimbus

■ One pair size 7 (4.5mm) needles OR SIZE TO OBTAIN GAUGE

GAUGE
12 sts and 29 rows = 4"/10cm over pattern st using size 7 (4.5mm) needles. TAKE TIME TO CHECK GAUGE.

NOTE
Slip all sts purlwise.

SCARF
Cast on 20 sts.
Set-up row Sl 1, k to end.
Rep set-up row for 7 rows more.

BEG PATTERN ST
Row 1 Sl 1, knit 1, *M1, k2, k2tog, k2; rep from * to end.
Rows 2–8 Sl 1, k to end.
Row 9 Sl 1, k1, *M1, k3, drop 1 st, k2; rep from * to end.
Rows 10–16 Sl 1, k to end.
Row 17 Sl 1, k1, *k2tog, k2, M1, k2; rep from * to end.
Rows 18–24 Sl 1, k to end.
Row 25 Sl 1, k1, *drop 1 st, k2, M1, k3; rep from * to end.
Rows 26–32 Sl 1, k to end.
Rep rows 1–32 for pat st 17 times more.

Next row Bind off knitwise, dropping 5th, 6th, 11th, 12th, 17th, and 18th sts. To keep end from bunching, work bind-off as foll: pull up a long loop when working st before dropped sts, then drop the next 2 sts, k the foll st, and pass the long-looped st over to bind off, creating long horizontal strands at edge.

Block gently, stretching scarf widthwise to straighten dropped sts and ensure all dropped sts are unraveled. ■

Girl's or Boy's Pocket Cardi

Play with color to create a cardigan that's just right for any little one, with patch pockets and a sweet collar shaped with short rows.

Designed by Sandi Rosner

SIZES

6 months (12 months, 18 months, 24 months)
Shown in size 12 months

KNITTED MEASUREMENTS

Chest (buttoned) 19 (20, 20¾, 22)"/48 (51, 52.5, 56)cm
Length 8½ (9, 9½, 10)"/21.5 (23, 24, 25.5)cm

MATERIALS

Girl's version
■ One 3½oz/100g skein (each approx 220yd/201m) of Universal Yarn *Deluxe Worsted Superwash* (100% wool) each in #729 neutral grey (A), #724 starfish (pink, B), and #741 heather (purple, C)

Boy's version
■ One 3½oz/100g skein (each approx 220yd/201m) of Universal Yarn *Deluxe Worsted Superwash* (100% wool) each in #731 burrow (A), #732 icy grey (B), and #714 petrol blue (C)

Both versions
■ Size 7 (4.5mm) circular needle, 24"/60cm long, OR SIZE TO OBTAIN GAUGE

■ Five ⅝"/15mm buttons

■ Stitch markers, stitch holder

GAUGE

18 sts and 36 rows = 4"/10cm over garter st using size 7 (4.5mm) needles.
TAKE TIME TO CHECK GAUGE.

SHORT ROW WRAP & TURN (W&T)

on RS row (on WS row)
1) Wyib (wyif), sl next st purlwise.
2) Move yarn between the needles to the front (back).
3) Sl the same st back to LH needle. Turn work. One st is wrapped.
4) When working the wrapped st, insert RH needle under the wrap and work it tog with the corresponding st on needle to hide or close wrap.

BUTTONHOLES

Girl's version
Buttonholes are worked at the beg of RS rows, as foll:
Row 1 (RS) Sl 1, k1, ssk, yo, k to end.
Row 2 (WS) Sl 1, k to end.
Row 3 Sl 1, k2, k into yo 2 rows below, k to end.

Boy's version
Buttonholes are worked at the end of RS rows, as foll:
Row 1 (RS) Sl 1, k to last 4 sts, yo, k2tog, k2.

Row 2 (WS) Sl 1, k to end.
Row 3 Sl 1, k to last 4 sts, k into yo 2 rows below, k3.

NOTES

1) Slip the first st of each row as if to purl, with yarn in front, to create a chain selvage.
2) Cardigan is worked back and forth in rows. Circular needle is used to accommodate large number of sts. Do not join.

BODY

With A, cast on 76 (80, 84, 88) sts.
Row 1 (WS) Sl 1, k to end.
Rows 2 and 3 Rep row 1.
Row 4 (buttonhole row RS) Work row 1 of buttonhole.
Cont in garter st, completing buttonhole, for 5 rows more. Break A and change to B.
Next row (inc RS) K5 (7, 9, 6), [M1, k5] 14 (14, 14, 16) times, k to end—90 (94, 98, 104) sts.
Cont in garter st with B for 5 rows more, then rep [6 rows C, 6 rows B] to end,
AT THE SAME TIME, work buttonhole on 3rd row of first C stripe, then every 16th (16th, 18th, 18th) row 3 times more,
AT THE SAME TIME, when piece measures 5 (5¼, 5½, 5¾)"/12.5 (13.5, 14, 14.5)cm from beg, end with a WS row.

DIVIDE FRONTS AND BACK

Next row (RS) Sl 1, k19 (20, 21, 21), bind off 8 (8, 8, 10) sts for right armhole, k34 (36, 38, 40) for back, bind off 8 (8, 8, 10) sts for left armhole, k to end. Cont on 20 (21, 22, 22) sts for left front only, work even in pat until armhole measures 2½ (2¾, 3, 3¼)"/6.5 (7, 7.5, 8)cm, end with a RS row.

SHAPE NECK

Bind off 5 sts at neck edge (beg of WS rows) once, 3 (4, 4, 4) sts once, 2 sts once. Dec 1 st at neck edge on foll row, then every other row once more—8 (8, 9, 9) sts. Work 1 WS row. Bind off.

RIGHT FRONT

Rejoin yarn to 20 (21, 22, 22) sts for right front at armhole edge, ready to work a WS row. Work even in pat until armhole measures 2½ (2¾, 3, 3¼)"/6.5 (7, 7.5, 8)cm, end with a WS row. Shape neck as for left front, reversing shaping by binding off at beg of RS rows.

BACK

Rejoin yarn to 34 (36, 38, 40) sts for back, ready to work a WS row. Work even in pat until armhole measures 3 (3¼, 3½, 3¾)"/7.5 (8, 9, 9.5)cm, end with a WS row.

SHAPE NECK

Next row (RS) K7 (7, 8, 8), k2tog, k1, join 2nd ball of yarn and bind off center 14 (16, 16, 18) sts, k1, ssk, k to end. Working both sides at once, dec 1 st at each neck edge every other row once. Work 1 WS row. Bind off rem 8 (8, 9, 9) sts each side.

SLEEVES

With A, cast on 22 (24, 26, 28) sts. Knit 9 rows. Cut A and change to B. Working in garter st, rep [6 rows B, 6 rows C] to end, AT THE SAME TIME, work as foll:
Knit 2 rows.
Inc row (RS) K2, M1, k to last 2 sts, M1, k2—2 sts inc'd.
Rep inc row every 6th (8th, 8th, 8th) row 5 times more—34 (36, 38, 40) sts. Work even until sleeve measures 6½ (7½, 8¾, 12)"/16.5 (19, 22, 30.5)cm from beg, end with a WS row and mark each end of last row for cap. Work even until piece measures 1 (1, 1, 1¼)"/2.5 (2.5, 2.5, 3)cm from markers. Bind off.

FINISHING

Sew shoulder seams. Sew sleeves into armholes, sewing caps above markers along bound-off edges of body. Sew sleeve seams. Sew buttons opposite buttonholes.

POCKETS

(make 2)
With A, cast on 13 (13, 15, 15) sts. Work in garter st until pocket measures 2 (2¼, 2½, 2¾)"/5 (5.5, 6.5, 7)cm. Bind off. Sew pockets to fronts approx 1½"/4cm from front edges, with lower edges aligned with last A row.

COLLAR

With RS facing and A, beg after 5-st bind-off, pick up and k 11 sts along right front neck edge to shoulder seam, place marker (pm), pick up and k 18 (20, 20, 22) sts along back neck edge, pm, pick up and k 11 sts along left neck edge, ending before 5 bound-off sts—40 (42, 42, 44) sts.
Row 1 (WS) Sl 1, k to 2nd marker at right shoulder seam, w&t.
Row 2 (RS) K to left shoulder seam marker, w&t.
Row 3 K to 3 sts past wrapped st from previous row, w&t.
Rows 4–6 Rep row 3.
Row 7 K to end of row.
Row 8 Sl 1, k to end.
Work 16 rows more in pat.
Bind off all sts. ■

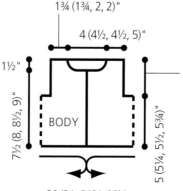

1¾ (1¾, 2, 2)"
4 (4½, 4½, 5)"
1½"
7½ (8, 8½, 9)"
BODY
3½ (3¾, 4, 4¼)"
5 (5¼, 5½, 5¾)"
20 (21, 21¾, 23)"

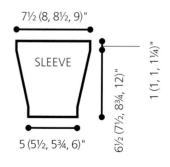

7½ (8, 8½, 9)"
SLEEVE
6½ (7½, 8¾, 12)"
1 (1, 1, 1¼)"
5 (5½, 5¾, 6)"

Fox Hood

Feel crazy like a fox in a playful, button-embellished cowl
with a hood that fits kids and adults alike.

◆

Designed by Tabetha Hedrick

SIZES
One size fits most

KNITTED MEASUREMENTS
Lower edge circumference 20"/51cm
Length 13½"/33cm

MATERIALS
■ Two 3½oz/100g skeins (each approx
220yd/201m) of Universal Yarn
Deluxe Worsted Superwash (100% wool)
in #702 autumn orange (A)

■ 1 skein each in #734 cream (B) and
#730 steel cut oats (C)

■ Size 11 (8mm) circular needle,
16"/40cm long, OR SIZE TO
OBTAIN GAUGE

■ Three ⅞"/22mm buttons

■ Small amount of fiberfill

■ Stitch marker

GAUGE
12 sts and 24 rows/rnds = 4"/10cm
over garter st using size 11 (8mm)
needles and 2 strands of yarn
held together.
TAKE TIME TO CHECK GAUGE.

NOTE

Piece is worked with 2 strands of yarn held together throughout. Lower edge is worked in rounds, then opening is created by working back and forth in rows to top of hood.

HOOD

With 2 strands of B held tog, cast on 60 sts. Join, taking care not to twist sts, and place marker (pm) for beg of rnd. Working in garter st (k 1 rnd, p 1 rnd), work 3 rnds B, 6 rnds C. Change to A and cont in garter st until cowl measures 5"/12.5cm from lower edge. Break yarn.

DIVIDE FOR OPENING

Sl 30 sts to LH needle, then rejoin double strand of B at center front and work back and forth in garter st (k every row) as foll:
Row 1 (RS) K1, ssk, k to last 3 sts, k2tog, k1—58 sts.
Row 2 (WS) Knit.
Bind off 2 sts at beg of next 4 rows—50 sts. Work even in garter st until opening measures 6"/15.5cm, end with a WS row.

BEG CHARTS

Row 1 (RS) Work chart A over 12 sts, work to last 12 sts, work chart B to end. Cont in pats as established through row 15 of charts. Bind off and seam top of hood.

OUTER EARS

(make 2)
With 2 strands of A, cast on 13 sts. Knit 6 rows.
Dec row (RS) Ssk, k to last 2 sts, k2tog—2 sts dec'd.
Cont in garter st, rep dec row every other row 3 times more—5 sts. Knit 1 row.
Next row (RS) K1, S2KP, k1—3 sts. Knit 1 row. Bind off.

INNER EARS

(make 2)
With 2 strands of B, cast on 11 sts. Work 6 rows in St st (k on RS, p on WS).
Dec row (RS) K1, ssk, k to last 3 sts, k2tog, k1—2 sts dec'd.
Cont in St st, rep dec row every other row twice more—5 sts. Purl 1 row.
Next row (RS) K1, S2KP, k1—3 sts. Purl 1 row. Bind off.

FINISHING

With RS together, sew inner ear to outer ear, leaving lower edge open. Turn RS out and stuff lightly. Sew lower edge, cinching to create curved shape. Using photo as guide, sew ears to each side of hood at an angle.

HOOD EDGING

With RS facing and 2 strands of B held tog, pick up and k 2 sts for every 3 rows around edge of opening. Join and pm for beg of rnd. Work 4 rnds in garter st. Bind off.

Sew 3 buttons to center front along first row of A. ∎

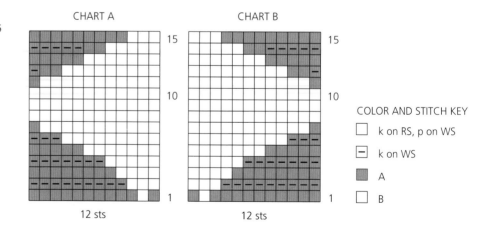

CHART A

CHART B

12 sts

12 sts

COLOR AND STITCH KEY

☐ k on RS, p on WS

⊟ k on WS

▧ A

☐ B

Short Row Ruffle Scarf

A wide scarf achieves balance with subtle short row shaping and a not-so-subtle contrast-color welted ruffle.

Designed by Ashley Rao

KNITTED MEASUREMENTS
7½ x 52"/19 x 132cm

MATERIALS
■ One 3½oz/100g skein (each approx 220yd/201m) of Universal Yarn *Deluxe Worsted* (100% wool) each in #31953 neutral grey (A) and #12298 butter (B)

■ One pair size 6 (4mm) needles OR SIZE TO OBTAIN GAUGE

GAUGE
18 sts and 32 rows = 4"/10cm over garter st using size 6 (4mm) needles. TAKE TIME TO CHECK GAUGE.

SHORT ROW WRAP & TURN (W&T)
on RS row (on WS row)
1) Wyib (wyif), sl next st purlwise.
2) Move yarn between the needles to the front (back).
3) Sl the same st back to LH needle. Turn work. One st is wrapped.
4) When working the wrapped st, insert RH needle under the wrap and work it tog with the corresponding st on needle to hide or close the wrap.

NOTE
When changing colors, twist strands on WS to prevent holes in work.

SCARF
With A, cast on 20 sts loosely; with B, cast on 13 sts loosely—33 sts.
Set-up row (WS) With B, k3, p10; with A, [k1, sl 2 sts purlwise wyif] twice, k to end.
Row 1 (RS) With A, sl 1 knitwise wyib, k15, sl 1 purlwise wyif, k2, sl 1 purlwise wyif; with B, k to end.
Row 2 (short row WS) With B, p10, w&t, k10.
Row 3 (WS) With B, p10, k3; with A, [k1, sl 2 sts purlwise wyif] twice, k to end.
Row 4 With A, sl 1 knitwise wyib, k15, sl 1 purlwise wyif, k2, sl 1 purlwise wyif; with B, k3, p10.
Row 5 (short row WS) With B, k10, w&t, p10.
Row 6 (WS) With B, k13; with A, [k1, sl 2 sts purlwise wyif] twice, k to end.
Rep rows 1–6 until piece measures 51½"/130.5cm from beg, measured along straight edge. Then, rep rows 1–4 once more. Bind off. ■

Colorblock Striped Infinity Scarf

Blocks of simple stripes make a striking statement in an easy scarf worked flat and joined at the ends to form a loop.

◆

Designed by Cheryl Murray

KNITTED MEASUREMENTS
Circumference 60"/152.5cm
Width 7"/18cm

MATERIALS
■ One 3½oz/100g skein (each approx 220yd/201m) of Universal Yarn *Deluxe Worsted Superwash* (100% wool) each in #733 sweatshirt grey (A), #702 autumn orange (B), #728 pulp (C), #745 cobalt (D), and #735 ebony (E)

■ One pair size 9 (5.5mm) needles OR SIZE TO OBTAIN GAUGE

■ Size G/6 (4mm) crochet hook

■ Scrap yarn for provisional cast-on

GAUGE
18 sts and 32 rows = 4"/10cm over garter st using size 9 (5.5mm) needles. TAKE TIME TO CHECK GAUGE.

PROVISIONAL CAST-ON
With scrap yarn and crochet hook, ch the number of sts to cast on plus a few extra. Cut a tail and pull the tail through the last chain. With knitting needle and yarn, pick up and knit the stated number of sts through the "purl bumps" on the back of the chain. To remove scrap yarn chain, when instructed, pull out the tail from the last crochet stitch. Gently and slowly pull on the tail to unravel the crochet stitches, carefully placing each released knit stitch on a needle.

3-NEEDLE BIND-OFF
1) Hold right sides of pieces together on 2 needles. Insert 3rd needle knitwise into first st of each needle, and wrap yarn knitwise.
2) Knit these 2 sts together, and slip them off the needles. *Knit the next 2 sts together in the same manner.
3) Slip first st on 3rd needle over 2nd st and off needle. Rep from * in step 2 across row until all sts are bound off.

SCARF
With A, cast on 32 sts using provisional cast-on.
[K 4 rows A, 4 rows B] 8 times.
[K 4 rows C, 4 rows B] 8 times.
[K 4 rows C, 4 rows D] 8 times.
[K 4 rows E, 4 rows D] 8 times.
[K 4 rows E, 4 rows A] 7 times, k 4 rows E.

[K 4 rows A, 4 rows B] 4 times.
[K 4 rows C, 4 rows B] 4 times.
[K 4 rows C, 4 rows D] 4 times.
[K 4 rows E, 4 rows D] 4 times.
[K 4 rows E, 4 rows A] 3 times, k 4 rows E.

Remove provisional cast-on and place 32 sts on needle. With E, join ends using 3-needle bind-off. ■

Felted Button Slippers

These snuggly, structured slippers are worked in one piece
in garter stitch and sewn together before felting.

♦

Designed by Kristina Tucker

◀▬■■□

KNITTED MEASUREMENTS
Circumference at toe 9"/23cm
Length 9"/23cm

MATERIALS
■ Two 3½oz/100g skeins (each approx
220yd/201m) of Universal Yarn
Deluxe Worsted (100% wool) in #12504
pomegranate heather

■ One pair size 11 (8mm) needles
OR SIZE TO OBTAIN GAUGE

■ Two ⅞"/22mm buttons

GAUGE
12 sts and 20 rows = 4"/10cm
over garter st before felting, using size
11 (8mm) needles and 2 strands
of yarn held tog.
TAKE TIME TO CHECK GAUGE.

MACHINE FELTING
1) Use a low water setting and
hottest temperature in a top-loading
washing machine. Add small amount
of laundry detergent and jeans or
towels for agitation.
2) Place item in a lingerie bag or zippered
pillowcase and add to machine. Check
the felting progress frequently, removing
item when the individual stitches are no
longer visible and item is felted to the
desired size.
3) Place item in cool water to stop the
felting process and remove suds. Remove
from lingerie bag and roll gently in towel
to remove excess water.
4) Block and shape while wet. Pin into
shape or stuff with plastic bags, and allow
to air dry completely.

NOTE
Slippers are worked with 2 strands of
yarn held tog throughout.

SLIPPERS
SOLE
With 2 strands of yarn held tog, cast
on 14 sts.
Work 56 rows in garter st (k every row).

UPPER
Using backward loop cast-on method, cast
on 23 sts at beg of next 2 rows—60 sts.
Work 22 rows in garter st. Bind off. Piece
will resemble a large letter "T."

FINISHING
Fold side edges of T shape down and
sew to base of T (the cast-on edge),
overlapping left over right side for
left slipper and vice versa, to form the
slipper. Sew overlapped edges for
approx 2½"/6.5cm from corner of toe.
Sew sole seams.
Machine or hand felt slippers. Sew buttons
to upper just below crossover point, using
photo as guide. ■

Garter & Lace Cowl

This neckwarmer knits up in a flash but doesn't skimp on style, with a tilted-blocks motif of garter stitch and lace that creates zigzag edges.

◆

Designed by Cheryl Murray

KNITTED MEASUREMENTS
Circumference 24"/61cm
Length 11"/28cm

MATERIALS
■ One 3½oz/100g skein (each approx 220yd/201m) of Universal Yarn *Deluxe Worsted* (100% wool) in #12188 heather

■ Size 8 (5mm) circular needle, 16"/40cm long, OR SIZE TO OBTAIN GAUGE

■ Stitch marker

GAUGE
16 sts and 32 rows = 4"/10cm after blocking, over pat st using size 8 (5mm) needle.
TAKE TIME TO CHECK GAUGE.

COWL
Cast on 96 sts. Join, taking care not to twist sts, and place marker (pm) for beg of rnd. [K 1 rnd, p 1 rnd] twice.

BEGIN PAT ST
Rnd 1 *K8, [yo, ssk] 4 times; rep from * around.
Rnd 2 *P8, k8; rep from * around.
Rnds 3, 5, 7, 9, and 11 Rep rnd 1.

Rnds 4, 6, 8, 10, and 12 Rep rnd 2.
Rnd 13 *[K2tog, yo] 4 times, k8; rep from * around.
Rnd 14 *K8, p8; rep from * around.
Rnds 15, 17, 19, 21, and 23 Rep rnd 13.
Rnds 16, 18, 20, 22, and 24 Rep rnd 14.
Rep rnds 1–24 for pat st twice more.

K 1 rnd, p 1 rnd, k 1 rnd.
Bind off loosely purlwise.

FINISHING
Block to measurements, pinning to create points along upper and lower edges. ■

Colorful Carryall Tote

Sturdy felted fabric, a canvas lining, and a plastic base make this bag eminently useful, and bright stripes add a dose of summer style.

Designed by Linda Cyr

KNITTED MEASUREMENTS

Approx 14 x 12 x 7"/35.5 x 30.5 x 18cm, after felting

MATERIALS

■ Two 3½oz/100g skeins (each approx 220yd/201m) of Universal Yarn *Deluxe Worsted* (100% wool) in #14007 indigo (G)

■ 1 skein each in #14006 raspberry (A), #12270 natural (B), #71662 turquoise (C), #12224 chartreuse olive (D), #12298 butter (E), and #14002 pumpkin (F)

■ One pair size 8 (5mm) needles OR SIZE TO OBTAIN GAUGE

■ Size 8 (5mm) circular needle, 32"/80cm long

■ 1yd/1m cotton canvas

■ 12 x 7"/30.5 x 18cm piece of stiff plastic (for base)

■ Sewing needle and thread

■ Stitch marker

GAUGE

16 sts and 34 rows = 4"/10cm over garter st using size 8 (5mm) needles, before felting.
TAKE TIME TO CHECK GAUGE.

MACHINE FELTING

1) Use a low water setting and hottest temperature in a top-loading washing machine. Add a small amount of laundry detergent and jeans or towels for agitation.
2) Place item in a lingerie bag or zippered pillowcase and add to machine. Check the felting progress frequently, removing item when the individual stitches are no longer visible and item is felted to the desired size.
3) Place item in cool water to stop the felting process and remove suds. Remove from lingerie bag and roll gently in towel to remove excess water.
4) Block and shape while wet. Pin into shape or stuff with plastic bags, and allow to air dry completely.

NOTE

Base of tote is worked in rows, then stitches are picked up around the base for the body of the toe, which is worked in rounds.

BASE

With G and straight needles, cast on 60 sts.
Next row (RS) Sl 1 wyif, k to end.
Cont in garter st (k every row), slipping first st of each row, until 72 rows are complete, end with a WS row. Change to circular needle.
Next rnd K60, pick up and k 35 sts along side edge, 60 sts along cast-on edge, 35 sts along side edge, place marker for beg of rnd—190 sts.
Work in garter st (k 1 rnd, p 1 rnd) until 20 rnds are complete, end with a purl rnd.

BODY OF TOTE

Cont in garter st, work in stripe sequence as foll: 6 rnds A, 4 rnds B, 4 rnds C, 4 rnds B, 8 rnds D, 6 rnds E, 4 rnds B, 8 rnds F, 4 rnds C, 4 rnds B, 6 rnds A, 8 rnds E, 6 rnds F, 4 rnds B, 6 rnds C, 6 rnds D, 4 rnds B, 8 rnds A, 6 rnds E, 4 rnds B, 6 rnds C, 4 rnds F. Bind off.

STRAPS

(make 4)
With G, cast on 10 sts.
Work in garter st, slipping first st of each row, for 68 rows. Bind off.

HANDLES
(make 2)
With G, cast on 10 sts. Work in garter st, slipping first st of each row, for 100 rows. Bind off.

FINISHING
Felt pieces by hand or machine.
Pin tote to measurements and let dry completely. Pin straps to 12"/30.5cm long and handles to 18"/45.5cm long and let dry completely.

LINING
Cut 2 pieces of canvas, each 20"/51cm wide and 18½"/47cm long. Place right sides tog and sew along sides and bottom, leaving ½"/1.5cm seam allowance. Turn top edge to WS for 1"/2.5cm and sew in place. Cut a 3"/7.5cm square out of each bottom corner to form base. Pin base seam in place, matching to side seams. Sew bottom seam, leaving ½"/1.5cm seam allowance. Sew sides of base to sides of lining. Place lining in tote. Sew in place along top edge. Wrap plastic in canvas and sew in place. Place inside tote.

Center 2 straps to each side of tote 5½"/14cm apart and sew in place. Line handles with canvas and sew to straps. ■

Corded Scarf

Twists of I-cord are worked into the surface of a simply shaped scarf
and looped at the ends for a one-of-a-kind style.

Designed by Kim Haesemeyer

KNITTED MEASUREMENTS
Approx 6 x 72"/15 x 183cm
without edgings

MATERIALS
■ Two 3½oz/100g skeins (each
approx 220yd/201m) of Universal
Yarn *Deluxe Worsted* (100% wool)
in #12277 periwinkle

■ One pair size 6 (4mm) needles
OR SIZE TO OBTAIN GAUGE

■ One set (5) size 6 (4mm)
double-pointed needles (dpns)

■ Size G/6 (4mm) crochet hook for
provisional cast-on

■ Stitch markers or small stitch holders

■ Scrap yarn

GAUGE
19 sts and 28 rows = 4"/10cm over
garter st using size 6 (4mm) needles.
TAKE TIME TO CHECK GAUGE.

PROVISIONAL CAST-ON

Using scrap yarn and crochet hook, ch the number of sts to cast on plus a few extra. Cut a tail and pull the tail through the last chain. With knitting needle and yarn, pick up and knit the stated number of sts through the "purl bumps" on the back of the chain. To remove scrap yarn chain, when instructed, pull out the tail from the last crochet stitch. Gently and slowly pull on the tail to unravel the crochet stitches, carefully placing each released knit stitch on a needle.

I-CORD

With 2 dpns, cast on 3 sts. *Knit one row. Without turning work, slide the sts back to the opposite end of needle to work next row from RS. Pull yarn tightly from the end of the row. Rep from * until I-cord is desired length.

SCARF

Cast on 28 sts using provisional cast-on.
Rows 1–5 Knit.
Row 6 (RS) K2, [kfb] 3 times, k3, [kfb] 3 times, k to end—34 sts.
Row 7 (WS) Knit, placing inc'd sts on st markers and holding them to back of work—28 sts, 6 sts on st markers.

BEGIN SURFACE I-CORDS

On RS of work, place held sts 1–3 on a dpn. Join a new ball of yarn and work a 3-st I-cord for 8"/20.5cm, leave sts on hold on dpn. Place held sts 4–6 on a 2nd dpn, work a 2nd I-cord for 7"/18cm, leave sts on hold on dpn.
Return to 28 scarf sts and cont in garter st (k every row) for 58 rows, end with a WS row.
Twist I-cords together approx 3 times, then join to body of scarf as foll:

Joining row (RS) K17, holding dpn with sts 4–6 parallel with needle, [k next scarf st tog with next st on dpn] 3 times, k3, holding dpn with sts 1–3 parallel with needle, [k next scarf st tog with next st on dpn] 3 times, k2.
Knit 5 rows, end with a WS row.
Next row (RS) K17, [kfb] 3 times, k3, [kfb] 3 times, k2.
Next row (WS) Knit, placing inc'd sts on st markers and holding them to back of work—28 sts, 6 sts on st holders.
On RS of work, place held sts 1–3 on a dpn. Join a new ball of yarn and work a 3-st I-cord for 7"/18cm, leave sts on hold on dpn. Place held sts 4–6 on a 2nd dpn, work a 2nd I-cord for 8"/20.5cm, leave sts on hold on dpn.
Return to 28 scarf sts and cont in garter st (k every row) for 58 rows, end with a WS row.
Twist I-cords together approx 3 times, then join to body of scarf as foll:
Joining row (RS) K2, holding dpn with sts 4–6 parallel with needle, [k next scarf st tog with next st on dpn] 3 times, k3, holding dpn with sts 1–3 parallel with needle, [k next scarf st tog with next st on dpn] 3 times, k to end.**
Rep from ** to ** 3 times more. Knit 6 rows. Leave sts on hold on needle for edging.

FINISHING
I-CORD EDGING

Working from the WS, place sts 1–3 on dpn. Work a 3-st I-cord for 8"/20.5cm, place sts on hold. Place sts 4–6 on dpn and work 2nd I-cord same as the first. Place sts 7–9 on dpn and work a 3-st I-cord for 6"/15cm, place sts on hold. Place sts 10–12 on dpn and work a 4th I-cord same as the 3rd.
Twist 3rd and 4th I-cords approx 5 times, then place all 6 sts from both cords on same dpn with 3rd cord sts to the right

of 4th cord sts. Twist 1st and 2nd I-cords approx 5 times, then place all 6 sts from both cords on same dpn with 2nd cord sts to the right of 1st cord sts.
Join yarn to edge and bind off sts 13–16, then join dpn with 3rd cord and 4th cord, then dpn with 1st cord and 2nd cord, binding off as the sts are joined, as foll:
K next edge st tog with next st on dpn, *k next edge st tog with next st on dpn, pass previous st on RH needle over st; rep from * to end, fasten off last st.

Remove provisional cast-on and carefully place live sts on needle to work edging at cast-on edge. Join yarn with RS facing and knit 1 row. Work edging as for opposite end.

Block gently. ◼

Button-Top Pincushions

These cute and useful pincushions, worked in a variety of tonal color palettes, are shaped with short rows and topped with a matching button.

◆

Designed by Nicole Feller-Johnson

KNITTED MEASUREMENTS
Finished diameter approx 6"/15cm
Finished height approx 3"/7.5cm

MATERIALS
■ Small amounts (approx 12yd/12m) from 3½oz/100g skeins (each approx 220yd/201m) of Universal Yarn *Deluxe Worsted* (100% wool) in each of 4 colors

Colorway 1 (corals):
#12256 tangerine flash (A), #13001 autumn orange (B), #3620 coral (C), and #91468 sunkist coral (D)

Colorway 2 (greens):
#12507 shamrock heather (A), #12285 cactus (B), #61633 greenery (C), and #12224 chartreuse olive (D)

Colorway 3 (blues):
#71662 turquoise (A), #12176 teal viper (B), #3669 Caribbean sea, and #12279 blue lagoon (D)

■ One pair size 2 (2.75mm) needles OR SIZE TO OBTAIN GAUGE

■ Two ⅞"/22mm buttons in coordinating colors for each pincushion

■ 1-quart ziplock bag for each pincushion

■ ⅓ quart of sawdust (or other stuffing material) for stuffing

■ Sharp darning needle

GAUGE
24 sts and 32 rows = 4"/10cm over garter st using size 2 (2.75mm) needles.
TAKE TIME TO CHECK GAUGE.

NOTE
It is not necessary to wrap short rows when working in garter st.

PINCUSHION
With A, cast on 30 sts.
Rows 1 and 2 Knit.
Row 3 K27, turn, k24, turn, k18, turn, k12, turn, k9, turn, k6, turn, k7, turn, k8, turn, k11, turn, k14, turn, k17, turn, k20, turn, k23, turn, k26, turn, k28, turn, k30. Do not break yarn.
Change to B.
Rep rows 1–3. Do not break yarn. Work 6 segments more, working rows 1–3 for each segment, in foll color sequence: C, D, A, B, C, D.
With D, bind off. Break all yarns, and weave in ends. Do not block. Sew cast-on edge to bound-off edge.

FINISHING
Sew hole at bottom of cushion closed. Sew button to cover closed hole. Fill ziplock bag with sawdust and zip closed. Gently ease bag of sawdust through opening at top of pincushion. Knead gently to distribute stuffing evenly. Sew top hole closed. Sew 2nd button to top. With sharp darning needle and strand of any color, sew through all layers from top button to bottom button and back several times, pulling tightly to cause the buttons to dimple the pincushion.

Cut length of yarn of any color and wrap clockwise around bottom button. Align yarn along color change between segments, pull tight and wrap top button one full turn clockwise, align yarn along color change directly opposite, pull tight and wrap around bottom button. Cont in this manner until all segments have been wrapped. Fasten off. ■

Blue Ice Wrap

Cool tones of blue and winter white lend a modern vibe to a striped wrap with seed stitch borders and a collar.

Designed by Galina Carroll

KNITTED MEASUREMENTS
Approx 19 x 52"/48 x 132cm

MATERIALS
■ One 3½oz/100g skein (each approx 220yd/201m) of Universal Yarn *Deluxe Worsted* (100% wool) each in #14016 ice flow (A), #12280 blue chic (B), #14008 cumulonimbus (C), and #12189 baby blue (D)

■ One pair size 8 (5mm) needles OR SIZE TO OBTAIN GAUGE

■ Small hook and eye set

GAUGE
16 sts and 24 rows = 4"/10cm over garter st using size 8 (5mm) needles. TAKE TIME TO CHECK GAUGE.

SEED STITCH
(over an odd number of sts)
Row 1 (RS) K1, *p1, k1; rep from * to end.
Row 2 K the purl sts and p the knit sts.
Rep row 2 for seed st.

NOTE
Carry yarns not in use along side edge, twist with working color at beg of RS rows to create a smooth edge. This smooth edge will be the lower edge of the wrap; sew collar to opposite long edge.

WRAP
With B, cast on 75 sts. Work 22 rows in seed st. With A, work 2 rows in seed st. Working in garter st (k every row), work stripe sequence as foll:
4 rows C, 2 rows A, 6 rows D, 2 rows B, 6 rows D, 2 rows A, 4 rows C, 10 rows A, 4 rows B, 2 rows A, 4 rows B, 10 rows A, 10 rows C, 10 rows A, 4 rows D, 4 rows C, 4 rows B, 4 rows D, 4 rows C, 8 rows B, 4 rows C, 4 rows D, 4 rows B, 4 rows C, 4 rows D.
Work 10 rows A, then work stripe sequence in reverse, beg with 4 rows D and working to 4 rows C. When reverse stripe sequence is complete, with A, work 2 rows in seed st, with B, work 22 rows in seed st. Bind off.

COLLAR
With B, cast on 90 sts. Work 8 rows in seed stitch. Working in garter st, work 4 rows A, 6 rows C, 10 rows D. Bind off. Center collar along long edge of wrap and sew in place. Sew hook and eye set to edge of wrap at base of collar. ■

Mosaic Diamonds Throw

Draw colorful inspiration from this showstopping blanket, knit in four strips and sewn together, with five complementary hues popping against a black background.

Designed by Susan Lowman

KNITTED MEASUREMENTS
Approx 40 x 44"/101.5 x 111.5cm

MATERIALS
■ Six 3½oz/100g skeins (each approx 220yd/201m) of Universal Yarn *Deluxe Worsted* (100% wool) in #1900 ebony (A)

■ 1 skein each in #3669 Carribean sea (B), #71662 turquoise (C), #91477 red oak (D), #3620 coral (E), and #41795 nectarine (F)

■ One pair size 7 (4.5mm) needles OR SIZE TO OBTAIN GAUGE

GAUGE
22 sts and 48 rows = 4"/10cm over mosaic pat using size 7 (4.5mm) needles.
TAKE TIME TO CHECK GAUGE.

MOSAIC PATTERN
(multiple of 6 sts plus 1; odd-numbered rows are RS rows)
Rows 1 and 2 With CC, k1, *sl 2, k1; rep from * to end.
Rows 3 and 4 With A, k3, sl 1, *k5, sl 1; rep from * to last 3 sts, k3.
Rows 5 and 6 With CC, sl 2, k3, *sl 3, k3; rep from * to last 2 sts, sl 2.
Rows 7 and 8 With A, k2, sl 3, *k3, sl 3; rep from * to last 2 sts, k2.
Rows 9 and 10 With CC, sl 1, *k5, sl 1; rep from * to end.
Rows 11 and 12 With A, k1, *sl 2, k1; rep from * to end.
Rows 13 and 14 With CC, k3, sl 1, *k5, sl 1; rep from * to last 3 sts, k3.
Rows 15 and 16 With A, sl 2, k3, *sl 3, k3; rep from * to last 2 sts, sl 2.
Rows 17 and 18 Rep rows 13 and 14.
Rows 19 and 20 Rep rows 11 and 12.
Rows 21 and 22 Rep rows 9 and 10.
Rows 23 and 24 Rep rows 7 and 8.
Rows 25 and 26 Rep rows 5 and 6.
Rows 27 and 28 Rep rows 3 and 4.
Rows 29 and 30 Rep rows 1 and 2.
Rows 31 and 32 With A, sl 1, *k5, sl 1; rep from * to end.
Rows 33 and 34 With CC, k2, sl 3, *k3, sl 3; rep from * to last 2 sts, k2.
Rows 35 and 36 Rep rows 31 and 32.
Rep rows 1–36 for mosaic pat.

COLOR SEQUENCE
STRIP 1
E, F, B, C, D.

STRIP 2
C, D, E, F, B.

STRIP 3
F, B, C, D, E.

STRIP 4
D, E, F, B, C.

NOTES
1) All sts are slipped purlwise with yarn held to WS of work.
2) A is the main color for all mosaic squares. CC is worked in the appropriate color (B, C, D, E, or F) for the color sequence.
3) Throw is worked in 4 strips of mosaic squares with short row borders and sewn together.
4) A 4-st garter st border is worked at beg of RS rows on each strip. Sts are knit with color A at beg of RS rows in which mosaic pat is worked with CC, and at ends of WS rows worked with A.

STRIP 1
With A, cast on 54 sts. Knit 6 rows.

SQUARE 1

Next row (RS) K4 A for border; with E, work row 1 of mosaic pat over 49 sts, k1.

Next row (WS) K1, work row 2 of mosaic pat to last 4 sts, turn.

Next row (RS) Work row 3 of mosaic pat, k1.

Next row (WS) K1, work row 4 of mosaic pat, k4 for border.

Cont to work pat in this manner, working k4 A for border *only* at beg of RS rows in which mosaic pat is worked with CC, and at ends of WS rows worked with A, until row 36 of mosaic pat is complete. Rep rows 1–36 once more, then rows 1–30 once.

With A, knit 6 rows.

CONT STRIP 1

Working in color sequence for strip 1, work 4 more squares as for square 1.

STRIPS 2, 3, AND 4

Work as for strip 1 in color sequence for each strip.

FINISHING
LEFT BORDER

With A, cast on 5 sts. Work in garter st until piece measures same as strip 4 from beg.

With RS facing, sew left border to left edge of strip 4. Sew rem strips tog. ■

Helpful Information

Knitting Needles

U.S.	METRIC
0	2mm
1	2.25mm
2	2.75mm
3	3.25mm
4	3.5mm
5	3.75mm
6	4mm
7	4.5mm
8	5mm
9	5.5mm
10	6mm
10½	6.5mm
11	8mm
13	9mm
15	10mm
17	12.75mm
19	15mm
35	19mm

Abbreviations

approx	approximately
beg	begin(ning)
CC	contrasting color
ch	chain
cm	centimeter(s)
cn	cable needle
cont	continu(e)(ing)
dec	decreas(e)(ing)
dpn	double-pointed needle(s)
foll	follow(s)(ing)
g	gram(s)
inc	increas(e)(ing)
k	knit
k2tog	knit 2 sts tog (one st has been decreased)
LH	left-hand
lp(s)	loop(s)
m	meter(s)
mm	millimeter(s)
MC	main color
M1	make one st; with needle tip, lift strand between last st knit and next st on LH needle and knit into back of it
M1 p-st	make 1 purl st
oz	ounce(s)
p	purl
pat(s)	pattern(s)
pm	place marker
psso	pass slip stitch(es) over
rem	remain(s)(ing)
rep	repeat
RH	right-hand
RS	right side(s)
rnd(s)	round(s)
SKP	slip 1, knit 1, pass slip st over (one st has been decreased)
SK2P	slip 1, knit 2 tog, pass slip st over the knit 2 tog (two sts have been decreased)
S2KP	slip 2 sts tog, knit 1, pass 2 slip sts over knit 1 (two sts have been decreased)
sl	slip
sl st	slip stitch
ssk	slip 2 sts kwise, one at a time; insert tip of LH needle into front of these sts and knit them tog (one st has been decreased)
ssp	slip 2 sts kwise, one at a time, wyif, insert tip of LH needle into back of these sts and knit them tog (one stitch has been decreased)
sssk	slip 3 sts kwise, one at a time; insert tip of LH needle into front of these sts and knit them tog (two sts have been decreased)
st(s)	stitch(es)
St st	stockinette stitch
tbl	through back loop(s)
tog	together
WS	wrong side(s)
wyib	with yarn in back
wyif	with yarn in front
yd	yard(s)
yo	yarn over needle
*	repeat directions following *
[ ]	repeat directions inside brackets as many times as indicated

Glossary

as foll Work the instructions that follow.

bind off Used to finish an edge or segment. Lift the first stitch over the second, the second over the third, etc. (U.K.: cast off)

bind off in ribbing Work in ribbing as you bind off. (Knit the knit stitches, purl the purl stitches.) (U.K.: cast off in ribbing)

3-needle bind-off With the right side of the two pieces facing and the needles parallel, insert a third needle into the first stitch on each needle and knit them together. Knit the next two stitches the same way. Slip the first stitch on the third needle over the second stitch and off the needle. Repeat for three-needle bind-off.

cast on Placing a foundation row of stitches upon the needle in order to begin knitting.

decrease Reduce the stitches in a row (that is, knit 2 together).

hold to front (back) of work Usually refers to stitches placed on a cable needle that are held to the front (or back) of the work as it faces you.

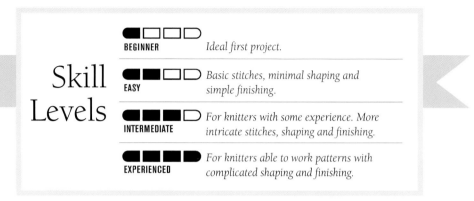

A NOTE ABOUT THE CHARTS
When working a chart in rows (knitting back and forth), right side rows are worked from right to left and wrong side rows from left to right.

When working a chart in rounds (knitting in the round), all rows are worked from right to left.

increase Add stitches in a row (that is, knit in front and back of stitch).

knitwise Insert the needle into the stitch as if you were going to knit it.

make one With the needle tip, lift the strand between the last stitch knit and the next stitch on the left-hand needle and knit into back of it. One knit stitch has been added.

make one p-st With the needle tip, lift the strand between the last stitch worked and the next stitch on the left-hand needle and purl it. One purl stitch has been added.

no stitch On some charts, "no stitch" is indicated with shaded spaces where stitches have been decreased or not yet made. In such cases, work the stitches of the chart, skipping over the "no stitch" spaces.

place markers Place or attach a loop of contrast yarn or purchased stitch marker as indicated.

pick up and knit (purl) Knit (or purl) into the loops along an edge.

purlwise Insert the needle into the stitch as if you were going to purl it.

selvedge stitch Edge stitch that helps make seaming easier.

slip, slip, knit Slip next two stitches knitwise, one at a time, to right-hand needle. Insert tip of left-hand needle into fronts of these stitches, from left to right. Knit them together. One stitch has been decreased.

slip, slip, slip, knit Slip next three stitches knitwise, one at a time, to right-hand needle. Insert tip of left-hand needle into fronts of these stitches, from left to right. Knit them together. Two stitches have been decreased.

slip stitch An unworked stitch made by passing a stitch from the left-hand to the right-hand needle as if to purl.

stockinette stitch Knit every right-side row and purl every wrong-side row.

work even Continue in pattern without increasing or decreasing. (U.K.: work straight)

work to end Work the established pattern to the end of the row.

Useful Techniques

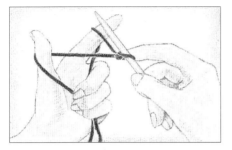

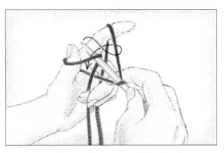

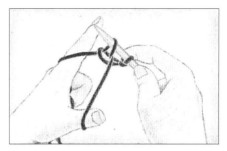

LONG-TAIL CAST-ON
1. Make a slip knot on the right needle, leaving a long tail. Wind the tail around your left thumb, front to back. Wrap the yarn from the ball over your left index finger and secure the ends in your palm.

2. Insert the needle upward in the loop on your thumb. Then, with the needle, draw the yarn from the ball through the loop to form a stitch.

3. Take your thumb out of the loop and tighten the loop on the needle. Continue in this way until all the stitches are cast on. ■

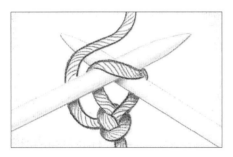

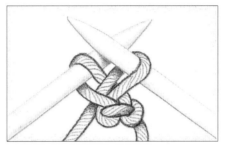

KNITTED-ON CAST-ON
1. Make a slip knot on the left needle. *Insert the right needle knitwise into the stitch on the left needle. Wrap the yarn around the right needle as if to knit.

2. Draw the yarn through the first stitch to make a new stitch, but do not drop the stitch from the left needle.

3. Slip the new stitch to the left needle as shown. Repeat from the * until the required number of stitches is cast on. ■

CABLE CAST-ON
1. Cast on 2 stitches using the knitted-on cast-on described on p. 131. *Insert the right needle between the two stitches on the left needle.

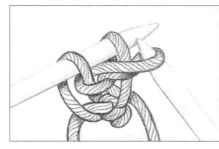

2. Wrap the yarn around the right needle as if to knit and pull the yarn through to make a new stitch.

3. Wrap the yarn around the right needle as if to knit and pull the yarn through to make a new stitch. ▮

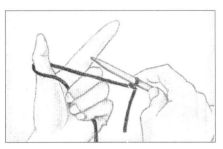

BACKWARD LOOP CAST-ON
1. Make a slip knot on the right needle, leaving a short tail. Wrap the yarn from the ball around your left thumb from front to back and secure it in your palm with your other fingers.

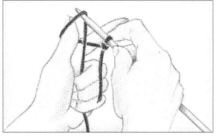

2. Insert the needle upward through the strand on your thumb.

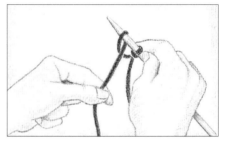

3. Slip this loop from your thumb onto the needle, pulling the yarn from the ball to tighten it. Continue in this way until all the stitches are cast on. ▮

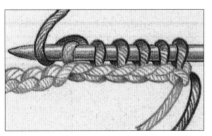

CHAIN-STITCH PROVISIONAL CAST-ON With waste yarn, make a crochet chain a few stitches longer than the number of stitches to be cast on. With main-color yarn, pick up one stitch in the back loop of each chain. To knit from the cast-on edge, carefully unpick the chain, placing the live stitches one by one on a needle. ▮

3-NEEDLE BIND-OFF

Double
Stitch
Cowl
_____
page 52

1. With the right sides of the two pieces facing each other, and the needles parallel, insert a third needle knitwise into the first stitch of each needle. Wrap the yarn around the needle as if to knit.

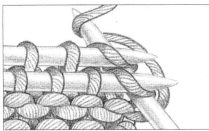

2. Knit these two stitches together and slip them off the needles. *Knit the next two stitches together in the same way as shown.

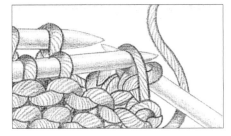

3. Slip the first stitch on the third needle over the second stitch and off the needle. Repeat from the * in step 2 across the row until all the stitches are bound off. ▧

◆ KITCHENER STITCH (GRAFTING)

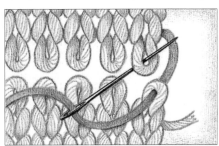

1. Insert the yarn needle purlwise into the first stitch on the front piece, then knitwise into the first stitch on the back piece.

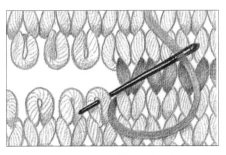

3. Insert the yarn needle purlwise into the next stitch on the front piece. Draw the yarn through.

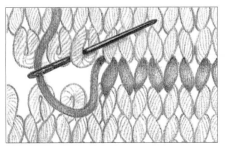

5. Insert the yarn needle knitwise into the next stitch on the back piece. Draw the yarn through. Repeat steps 2 through 5. ▧

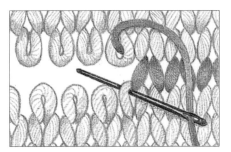

2. Insert the yarn needle knitwise into the first stitch on the front piece again. Draw the yarn through.

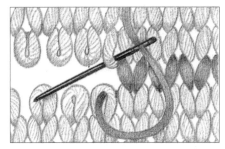

4. Insert the yarn needle purlwise into the first stitch on the back piece again. Draw the yarn through.

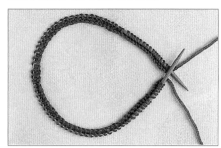

CIRCULAR NEEDLES

1. Cast on as you would for straight knitting. Distribute the stitches evenly around the needle, being sure not to twist them. The last cast-on stitch is the last stitch of the round. Place a marker here to indicate the end of the round.

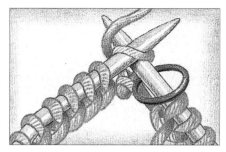

2. Hold the needle tip with the last cast-on stitch in your right hand and the tip with the first cast-on stitch in your left hand. Knit the first cast-on stitch, pulling the yarn tight to avoid a gap.

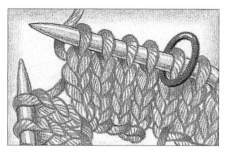

3. Work until you reach the marker. This completes the first round. Slip the marker to the right needle and work the next round. ∎

DOUBLE-POINTED NEEDLES

1. Cast on with three needles.

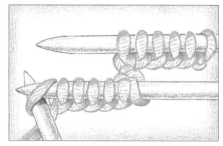

2. Cast on the required number of stitches on the first needle, plus one extra. Slip this extra stitch to the next needle, as shown. Continue in this way, casting on the required number of stitches on the last needle.

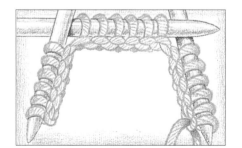

3. Arrange the needles as shown, with the cast-on edge facing the center of the triangle (or square).

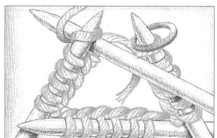

4. Place a stitch marker after the last cast-on stitch. With the free needle, knit the first cast-on stitch, pulling the yarn tightly. Continue knitting in rounds, slipping the marker before beginning each round. ∎

Simply Striped Mitts

page 24

ALONG A HORIZONTAL EDGE

1. Insert the knitting needle into the center of the first stitch in the row below the bound-off edge. Wrap the yarn knitwise around the needle.

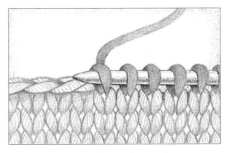

2. Draw the yarn through. You have picked up one stitch. Continue to pick up one stitch in each stitch along the bound-off edge. ■

Mitered Squares
Baby Blanket

page 32

ALONG A VERTICAL EDGE

1. Insert the knitting needle into the corner stitch of the first row, one stitch in from the side edge. Wrap the yarn around the needle knitwise.

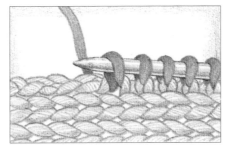

2. Draw the yarn through. You have picked up one stitch. Continue to pick up stitches along the edge. Occasionally skip one row to keep the edge from flaring. ■

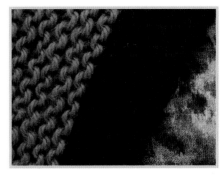

Contrast Band Capelet

page 40

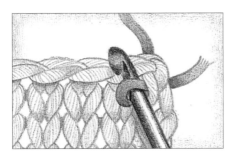

WITH A CROCHET HOOK

1. Insert the crochet hook from front to back into the center of the first stitch one row below the bound-off edge. Catch the yarn and pull a loop through.

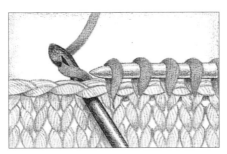

2. Slip the loop onto the knitting needle, being sure it is not twisted. Continue to pick up one stitch in each stitch along the bound-off edge. ■

CABLES

Note: Cables shown are 6-stitch cables (3 sts on each side). Twists are made with 2 stitches (1 on each side). Stitch glossaries in each pattern specify stitch counts for cables used in that pattern.

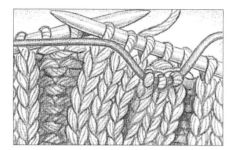

FRONT (OR LEFT) CABLE
1. Slip the first 3 stitches of the cable purlwise to a cable needle and hold them to the front of the work. Be careful not to twist the stitches.

2. Leave the stitches suspended in front of the work, keeping them in the center of the cable needle where they won't slip off. Pull the yarn firmly and knit the next 3 stitches.

3. Knit the 3 stitches from the cable needle. If this seems too awkward, return the stitches to the left needle and then knit them. ■

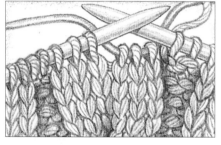

BACK (OR RIGHT) CABLE
1. Slip the first 3 stitches of the cable purlwise to a cable needle and hold them to the back of the work. Be careful not to twist the stitches.

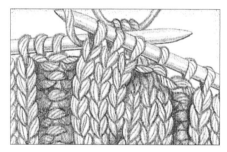

2. Leave the stitches suspended in back of the work, keeping them in the center of the cable needle where they won't slip off. Pull the yarn firmly and knit the next 3 stitches.

3. Knit the 3 stitches from the cable needle. If this seems too awkward, return the stitches to the left needle and then knit them. ■

YARN OVERS

A yarn over is a decorative increase made by wrapping the yarn around the needle.
There are various ways to make a yarn over depending on where it is placed.

BETWEEN TWO KNIT STITCHES
Bring the yarn from the back of the work
to the front between the two needles. Knit
the next stitch, bringing the yarn to the
back over the right needle as shown. ▪

**BETWEEN A KNIT AND A PURL
STITCH** Bring the yarn from the back to
the front between the two needles, then to
the back over the right needle and to the
front again as shown. Purl the next stitch.▪

**BETWEEN A PURL AND A KNIT
STITCH** Leave the yarn at the front of
the work. Knit the next stitch, bringing the
yarn to the back over the right needle
as shown. ▪

BETWEEN TWO PURL STITCHES
Leave the yarn at the front of the work.
Bring the yarn to the back over the right
needle and to the front again as shown.
Purl the next stitch. ▪

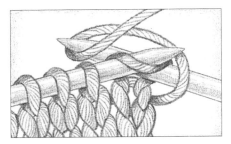

AT THE BEGINNING OF A KNIT ROW
Keep the yarn at the front of the work.
Insert the right needle knitwise into the first
stitch on the left needle. Bring the yarn
over the right needle to the back and knit
the next stitch, holding the yarn over
with your thumb if necessary. ▪

AT THE BEGINNING OF A PURL ROW
To work a yarn over at the beginning of a
purl row, keep the yarn at the back of the
work. Insert the right needle purlwise
into the first stitch on the left needle. Purl
the stitch. ▪

MULTIPLE YARN OVERS
1. For multiple yarn overs (two or more),
wrap the yarn around the needle as for a
single yarn over, then wrap the yarn
around the needle once more (or as many
times as indicated). Work the next stitch
on the left needle.

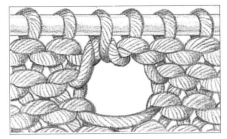

2. Alternate knitting and purling into
the multiple yarn over on the subsequent
row, always knitting the last stitch on a
purl row and purling the last stitch on
a knit row. ▪

Lacy
Heart
Shawl

page 43

137

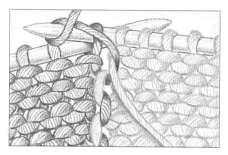

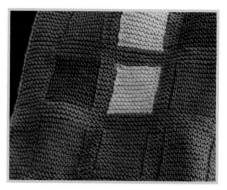

CHANGING COLORS ON A VERTICAL LINE

1. On the knit side, drop the old color. Pick up the new color from under the old color and knit to the next color change.

2. On the purl side, drop the old color. Pick up the new color from under the old color and purl to the next color change. Repeat steps 1 and 2. ■

Happy Blocks Baby Blanket

page 12

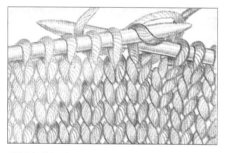

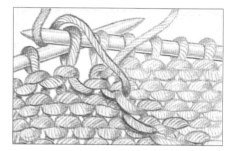

CHANGING COLORS ON A DIAGONAL LINE

1. When working a right diagonal on the knit side, bring the new color over the top of the old color and knit to the next color change.

2. On the purl side, pick up the new color from under the old color and purl to the next color change. ■

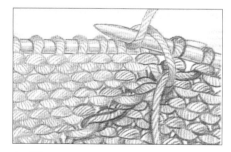

1. When working a left diagonal on the purl side, bring the new color over the top of the old color and purl to the next color change.

2. On the knit side, pick up the new color from under the old color and knit to the next color change. ■

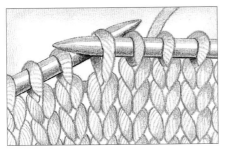

1. To prevent holes in the piece and create a smooth transition, wrap a knit stitch as follows: With the yarn in back, slip the next stitch purlwise.

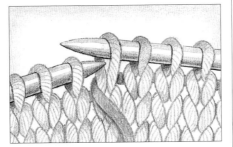

2. Move the yarn between the needle to the front of the work.

Cast on about three to five stitches. *Knit one row. Without turning the work, slip the stitches back to the beginning of the row. Pull the yarn tightly from the end of the row. Repeat from the * as desired. Bind off. ■

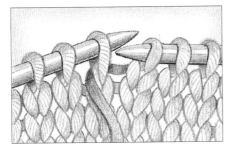

3. Slip the same stitch back to the left needle. Turn the work, bringing the yarn to the purl side between the needles. One stitch is wrapped.

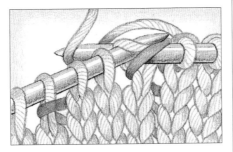

4. When you have completed all the short rows, you must hide the wraps. Work to just before the wrapped stitch. Insert the right needle under the wrap and knitwise into the wrapped stitch. Knit them together. ■

Corded Scarf

page 119

Button-Top Pincushions

page 122

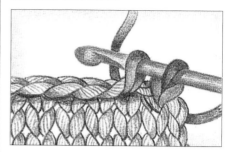

1. Draw the yarn through the loop on the hook by catching it with the hook and pulling it toward you.

2. One chain stitch is complete. Lightly tug on the yarn to tighten the loop if it is very loose, or wiggle the hook to loosen the loop if it is very tight. Repeat from step 1 to make as many chain stitches as required for your pattern.

1. Draw through a loop as for a slip stitch, bring the yarn over the hook, and pull it through the first loop. *Insert the hook into the next stitch and draw through a second loop.

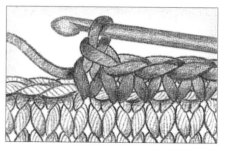

2. Yarn over and pull through both loops on the hook. Repeat from the * to the end. ■

3. To count the number of chain stitches made, hold the chain so that the Vs are all lined up. Do not count the loop on the hook or the slip knot you made when beginning the chain. Each V counts as one chain made. ▨

Eyelet Slippers

page 86

HOW TO MAKE A POMPOM

1. With two circular pieces of cardboard the width of the desired pompom, cut a center hole. Then cut a pie-shaped wedge out of the circle. (Use the picture as a guide.)

2. Tightly hold the two circles together and wrap the yarn tightly around the cardboard. Then carefully cut around the cardboard.

3. Tie a piece of yarn tightly between the two circles. Remove the cardboard and trim the pompom.

4. Sandwich pompom between two round pieces of cardboard held together with a long needle. Cut around the circumference for a perfect pompom. ∎

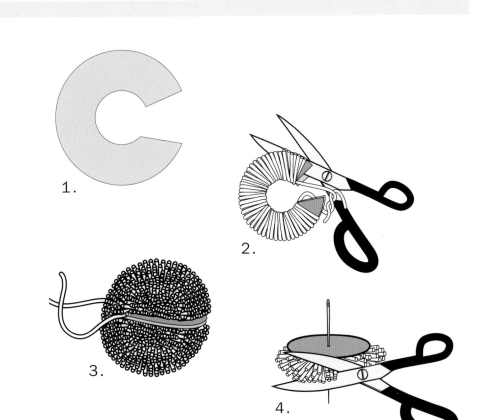

1.

2.

3.

4.

EMBROIDERY STITCHES

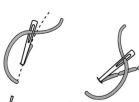

BACKSTITCH

RUNNING STITCH

CHAIN STITCH

FRENCH KNOT

STRAIGHT STITCH

About the Yarns

FABRIC CARE AND BLOCKING

Maintain the beauty and lasting warmth of projects made in Universal Yarn Deluxe Worsted (100% wool) 🧶 by following proper care guidelines. Hand wash all finished projects by submerging them in cold water with a small amount of gentle soap. Carefully wash the garment, being careful not to create too much friction, and rinse in cold water. Gently remove excess water and dry finished garments flat or on a blocking board. It is not recommended bleach or an iron be used on the yarn or fabric. Deluxe Worsted Superwash can be cared for by machine. Wash using warm water on a gentle cycle and dry on low.

WHERE TO FIND UNIVERSAL YARN DELUXE WORSTED

Visit the Universal Yarn website at www.UniversalYarn.com to see the full collection of colors and textures in the Deluxe Collection of wools, and to find a U.S.-based Deluxe Worsted and Deluxe Worsted Superwash retailer near you.

UNIVERSAL YARN
5991 Caldwell Park Drive
Harrisburg, NC 28075
Tel: 877.864.9276 / Fax: 704.455.1029
e-mail: sales@universalyarn.com
www.universalyarn.com

Standard Yarn Weight System
Categories of yarns, gauge ranges, and recommended needle and hook sizes

Yarn Weight Symbol & Category Names	0 Lace	1 Super Fine	2 Fine	3 Light	4 Medium	5 Bulky	6 Super Bulky
Type of Yarns in Category	Fingering 10 count crochet thread	Sock, Fingering, Baby	Sport, Baby	DK, Light Worsted	Worsted, Afghan, Aran	Chunky, Craft, Rug	Bulky, Roving
Knit Gauge Range* in Stockinette Stitch to 4 inches	33–40** sts	27–32 sts	23–26 sts	21–24 sts	16–20 sts	12–15 sts	6–11 sts
Recommended Needle in Metric Size Range	1.5–2.25 mm	2.25–3.25 mm	3.25–3.75 mm	3.75–4.5 mm	4.5–5.5 mm	5.5–8 mm	8 mm and larger
Recommended Needle U.S. Size Range	000 to 1	1 to 3	3 to 5	5 to 7	7 to 9	9 to 11	11 and larger
Crochet Gauge* Ranges in Single Crochet to 4 inch	32–42 double crochets**	21–32 sts	16–20 sts	12–17 sts	11–14 sts	8–11 sts	5–9 sts
Recommended Hook in Metric Size Range	Steel*** 1.6–1.4mm Regular hook 2.25 mm	2.25–3.5 mm	3.5–4.5 mm	4.5–5.5 mm	5.5–6.5 mm	6.5–9 mm	9 mm and larger
Recommended Hook U.S. Size Range	Steel*** 6, 7, 8 Regular hook B–1	B–1 to E–4	E–4 to 7	7 to I–9	I–9 to K–10½	K–10½ to M–13	M–13 and larger

* GUIDELINES ONLY: The above reflect the most commonly used gauges and needle or hook sizes for specific yarn categories.
** Lace weight yarns are usually knitted or crocheted on larger needles and hooks to created lacy openwork patterns. Accordingly, a gauge range is difficult to determine. Always follow the gauge stated in your pattern.
*** Steel crochet hooks are sized differently from regular hooks—the higher the number, the smaller the hook, which is the reverse of regular hook sizing. This Standards & Guidelines booklet and downloadable symbol artwork are available at: YarnStandards.com

---

CANADA
Diamond Yarn
155 Martin Ross Ave Unit 3
Toronto (Ont.) M3J2L9
Tel: 800.268.1896 / Fax: 416.736.6112
www.diamondyarn.com

MEXICO
Rebecca Pick Estambres
Lago Chalco No. 129 Col Anahuac
C.P. 1320 Mexico, D.F.
Tel: 52.5341.4413 / Fax: 52.5341.6019
www.rebeccapickestambres.com

TURKEY
Defne
Yeni Yalova Yolu Buttim Plaza
Kat. 19 No: 1663/Bursa
Tel: 90.224.221.0750 / Fax: 90.224.211.0753
e-mail: info@defneiplikpazarlama.com

Index

page 32

page 53

page 102

page 69

page 35

page 100